A Complaint Free World

A Complaint Free World

How to Stop Complaining and *Start Enjoying the Life* You Always Wanted

WILL BOWEN

DOUBLEDAY

New York   London   Toronto   Sydney   Auckland

PUBLISHED BY DOUBLEDAY

Published in the United States by Doubleday, an imprint of
The Doubleday Broadway Publishing Group, a division of
Random House, Inc., New York.
www.doubleday.com

DOUBLEDAY and the portrayal of an anchor with a dolphin are
registered trademarks of Random House, Inc.

Book design by Tina Henderson

Library of Congress Cataloging-in-Publication Data
Bowen, Will.
  A complaint free world : how to stop complaining and start
enjoying the life you always wanted / Will Bowen. — 1st ed.
      p. cm.
  1. Criticism, Personal. 2. Faultfinding. 3. Self-help techniques.
4. Life skills. 5. Performance—Psychological aspects. I. Title.
  BF637.C74B69 2007
  158.1—dc22

                                                2007030282

ISBN 978-0-385-52458-2

PRINTED IN THE UNITED STATES OF AMERICA

10 9 8 7 6 5 4 3 2 1

First Edition

For my daughter, Lia, her children yet to be, and their children; each of whom will live in a subsequently happier, more Complaint Free world.

CONTENTS

ACKNOWLEDGMENTS

Thank you to the beautiful people of Christ Church Unity, Kansas City, MO, and to the volunteers, donors, and supporters who have made the Complaint Free movement a reality. Thank you to my wife, Gail, for her unending love and encouragement. Thank you to my mom, Lindy, my dad, Bill, my brothers, Chuck and Dave, and my stepmother, Bobby, for always believing in me. Thank you to Steve Hanselman of Level 5 Media for being a sounding board, guide, and mentor. Thank you to Alice Anderson for modeling a life of principle and integrity. Thank you to Sallye Taylor, who has always believed in me and prodded me to be my best. Thank you to Terry Lund for her prayers. Thank you to Yakov Smirnoff, Dan Murphy, Chris de Leon, Steve Hall, Adam Khan, and Gary Hild for friendships that exist beyond time and distance. Thank you to Steve Rubin, Bill Barry, Trace Murphy, and the incredible staff at Doubleday. Thank you to Joe Jacobson for always being there.

And thank you, dear reader, for being open to a new paradigm for your life and, thereby, shining light into our world.

A Complaint Free World

" PURPLE ?! "

INTRODUCTION

If you don't like something, change it.
If you can't change it, change your attitude.
Don't complain.

—MAYA ANGELOU

I n your hands you hold the secret to transforming your life. Big words? Yes, but I've seen it work for many, many people. I've read their e-mails and letters and taken their phone calls. People have used the simple concept of putting a purple silicone bracelet on their wrist and then switching it from wrist to wrist until they have managed to go 21 consecutive days without complaining, criticizing, or gossiping. In so doing, they have formed a new habit. By becoming conscious of and, thereby, changing their words, they have changed their thoughts and begun to create their lives by design. People just like you have shared stories with me of chronic pain relieved, relationships healed, careers improved, and having become an overall happier person.

One man I know suffered from chronic headaches. Every night he would arrive home from work and tell his wife how much his head had hurt that day. Realizing that telling his wife about his headaches did nothing to lessen their occurrence or severity, he decided to stop talking about them as a part of becoming complaint free.

The man's name is Tom Alyea. He no longer has these headaches and he's now the senior coordinator of our Complaint Free World program, one of several dozens of volunteers who make this all happen.

Less pain, better health, satisfying relationships, a better job, being more serene and joyous . . . Sound good? It's not only possible, it's probable. Consciously striving to reformat your mental hard drive is not easy, but you can start now and in a short period of time—time that will pass anyway—you can have the life you've always dreamed of having.

You can order a purple Complaint Free bracelet by visiting our Web site: www.AComplaintFreeWorld.org. We send the bracelets out free (the program is supported entirely by donations and you can donate if you choose). Here is how to use the bracelet:

1. Begin to wear the bracelet on either wrist.
2. When you catch yourself complaining, gossiping, or criticizing, move the bracelet to the other wrist and begin again.
3. If you hear someone else who is wearing a purple bracelet complain, it's okay to point out their need to switch the bracelet to the other arm; BUT if you're going to do this, you must move your bracelet first! Because you're complaining about their complaining.
4. Stay with it. It may take many months to reach 21 consecutive days. The average is 4 to 8 months.

And relax. We're only talking about complaints, criticism, and gossip that is spoken. If it comes out of your mouth, it counts, so start over. If you think it, it's free. But you'll find out that even complaining thoughts will disappear as you move through this process.

Start right now. You don't have to wait for your purple bracelet to arrive to get started. Slip a rubber band on your wrist, put a coin or small stone in your pocket, move a paperweight to one side of your desk or find your own distinctive way of self-monitoring now. Do it now. Then, when you catch yourself complaining, criticizing, or gossiping, move the item. Move the rubber band to the other wrist, switch the coin to another pocket, or move the paperweight to the other side of the desk. It's important that you move the item. It's that act of moving it that plows furrows deeply into your consciousness, making you aware of your behavior. You must move it, every time.

Did you catch the very important word in the last paragraph? I said WHEN you catch yourself complaining, not IF. Complaining is epidemic in our world, so don't be surprised when you find out that you, too, gripe a lot more than you thought.

In this book you will learn what constitutes a complaint, why we complain, what benefits we think we receive from complaining, how complaining is destructive to our lives, and how we can get others around us to stop complaining. You will learn the steps to eradicating this poisonous form of expression from your life. If you stay with it, you will find that not only will you not complain, but others around you will cease to do so as well.

A while back, I was playing racquetball with a friend. Catching our breath between games, he asked, "So how many purple Complaint Free bracelets have you sent out?" "About one hundred twenty-five thousand," I responded, and then I added, "so far." Taking a moment for that to sink in, he sipped his water and said, "One hundred twenty-five thousand . . . that's more than the population of a good-sized American city." "Yeah," I said, still trying to wrap my head around it all. "And how long have you been at it?" he asked. "Seven months," I replied. "One hundred twenty-five thousand bracelets in seven months," he repeated, shaking his head in disbelief.

Adjusting his sweat bands and replacing his goggles for our final game of the day, he asked, "How many times a day do you think people complain?" "I don't know," I said. "When I first started trying to go 21 consecutive days without complaining, I was moving my own purple bracelet about 20 times a day." He stood, indicating he was ready to continue playing. Grabbing his racquet and giving it a few swings to keep his shoulder limber, he said, "Do the math." Wondering if somehow I'd miscalculated the score of our last game, I asked, "What math?"

"If you take 125,000 bracelets," he said, "and multiply that times twenty complaints per day, times thirty days each month, times seven months, you get . . . well, it's . . . well, it's a heck of a lot! Think how many complaints have NOT been made since this began." I stood a moment, thinking about this, and then walked on the racquetball court. He entered the court, approached the serving line, and launched one of his "death-in-a-corner" serves. My mind was preoccupied by his comment. I fanned the ball. I just couldn't stop thinking about what my friend had said, and ultimately he won the game. How much complaining, criticism, and gossip had this simple idea already helped prevent?

It certainly seemed be having an impact, and the idea was continuing to grow. The church staff, where I am the minister, was averaging 7,000 requests for Complaint Free purple bracelets a week. We had shipped them to eighty countries around the world. The mail folder that our office manager placed on my desk each week had swelled to a sheaf of letters nearly an inch thick. Schoolteachers were telling me that encouraging their students to become conscious of their complaining had transformed classrooms. Churches of various denominations were embracing this idea, not only giving "no-complaint" bracelets but beginning Complaint Free Wednesday-night classes and creating Complaint Free Sunday school curricula. People who were facing betrayal, poverty, life-threatening disease, job cuts, and even natural disasters were picking up the challenge to try to erase complaining from their lives.

This thing had taken on a life of its own, and it was thrilling to be a part of it.

In the summer of 2006, I decided to create a "Summer Book Club" at our church. We would encourage everyone to read the same book and have classes and discussions about what we were reading.

Wanting to select a book that would truly have an impact, we first looked at what our people needed. The number-one challenge people faced seemed to be money. Couples and singles alike came to talk to me about being in debt, job uncertainty, and feeling financially overwhelmed. After checking out several books on the subject, we selected *The Four Spiritual Laws of Prosperity* by

Edwene Gaines. Her book gives clear, concise, powerful, and measurable things one can do to begin to live a life of abundance. More than 100 people purchased the book, and I planned a five-week series in addition to classes for people to delve deeper and share their questions, ideas, and insights.

The second week of the series, I was in my home office writing my lesson when I had a moment of inspiration. I called Marcia Dale, our office manager.

I explained my idea to Marcia. She listened patiently, then sighed and said, "Another doodad Sunday?" Marcia feigned exasperation, but the truth is that she loves it when we give out little trinkets at classes and services. We've given out magnets, bookmarks, picture frames, pens, and other knickknacks that support and reinforce what we're learning. The "doodads," as Marcia calls them, serve as a visual reminder long after the lesson is completed.

"Why rubber bracelets?" she asked. I explained that Gaines's book, like many others, reminded us that it's important to focus on what we want in our lives rather than putting our attention on what we don't want. "Thoughts held in mind produce after their kind," Marcia said, echoing back something she'd heard hundreds of times. "Exactly," I said. "And complaining is focusing on what we don't want. It's talking about what's wrong, and what we focus our attention on expands. So we want to help people eradicate complaining from their lives, and this will serve as a great reinforcement."

"Tell me again how rubber bracelets will do this," Marcia said ambiguously. "We'll give everyone a bracelet; you know, like the LIVESTRONG bracelets distributed to raise money for the Lance Armstrong Foundation, but another color," I said. "About twenty years ago, I read a book that said it takes 21 days for a hen's egg to hatch and, ironically, it also takes 21 days of a person doing a new behavior for it to become a habit. We'll challenge everyone to put the bracelet on either arm and try to go 21 consecutive days without complaining. If they catch themselves complaining, we'll encourage them to move the bracelet to the other wrist and begin again."

"Ooo . . . sounds hard," Marcia observed. Then, looking for a loophole, she asked, "If they complain, can they start over the next day and just have a 'free day,' complaining all they want for the rest of that day?" "No," I said, "they switch the bracelet and start again at that moment. The idea is to make us aware of when we complain so, maybe, we catch ourselves before we do it next time."

The phone was silent for a moment. "Marcia?" I said, checking to see if our call had been dropped. "I'm here," she said flatly. "I'm just wondering if people can do this . . . heck, I'm wondering if I can do this!" "Me, too," I said. "Let's give it a try."

"Okay," she said ruefully, "I'll call some doodad places and see what I can find. Any particular color of bracelet?" I thought a moment. "No . . . what do you think?" I asked. "How about purple?" she said. "It's classy and to some people it represents transformation. Besides, you see yellow, orange, and pink bracelets everywhere, but not purple." "Sounds good," I said.

Marcia found a company that sold purple rubber bracelets with the word SPIRIT debossed in them and we agreed to order 500, more than twice what we needed—little did we know. When Marcia told me about the bracelets, I asked, "Why 'spirit'?" "It stands for 'school spirit,' I think," she said. "They sell 'em in all kinds of colors. If your school's color is orange, you buy orange 'spirit' bracelets. If your color is red, you buy red 'spirit' bracelets." "Oh," I said. "So we can't get bracelets that say something like 'no complaining' on them?" "We can," she answered, "but on an order of 500, the cost is out of sight. Besides, it's just a doodad most people will throw in a drawer as soon as they get home."

"How am I going to explain the word 'spirit' on them?" I wondered aloud. "Tell everybody it stands for 'the spirit of change,'" Marcia said, answering my question for me.

The next Sunday, we gave out just over 250 bracelets, but our entire stock of 500 was totally depleted right after the service from people wanting them for their offices, classes, friends, teams, and social groups. That day, in addition to explaining how the challenge works, I invited everyone to imagine what their lives would be like without the "ear pollution" of complaints. I could feel a mixture of excitement and trepidation in the room. I told them that I was accepting my own challenge and that, no matter how long it took, I was going to make it 21 consecutive days without complaining. "Twenty-one days in a row," I affirmed, "with no complaining, criticizing, or gossiping."

"Join me. If it takes three months or three years," I said, "your life will be greatly improved. If you wear your bracelet out from switching it back and forth, we'll give you another one. Stay with it."

Complaining is talking about things you do not want rather than what you do want. When we complain, we are using our words to focus on things that are not as we would like. Our thoughts create our lives and our words indicate what we are thinking. Let me repeat that, because if you get nothing else from this book, please let this be it: *OUR THOUGHTS CREATE OUR LIVES AND OUR WORDS INDICATE WHAT WE ARE THINKING.*

Put another way: "What you Articulate, you Demonstrate!"

We are, every one of us, already creating our lives all the time. The trick is to really take the reins and steer the horse to where we do want to go, rather than where we do not. Your life is a movie written by, directed by, produced by, and starring—you guessed it—YOU! We are all self-made. When asked about "self-made millionaires," Earl Nightingale, the twentieth-century motivational master and philosopher, once quipped, "We are all self-made, but only the successful will admit it."

You are creating your life in every moment with the thoughts to which you give the most attention. Today, people are waking up to this as never before, and it rings the bells of change for the consciousness of our world. Our collective minds are starting to the grasp that our lives, our society, our political situation, our health, and indeed the state of our world are an out-picturing of the thoughts we hold and the actions those thoughts produce.

This idea is anything but new. It seems to be reaching a critical mass in our universal understanding today, but thousands of great philosophers and teachers have told us this for millennia:

"As thou hast believed, so be it done unto thee."

—JESUS, MATTHEW 8:13

"The universe is change; our life is what our thoughts make it."

—MARCUS AURELIUS

"We are shaped by our thoughts; we become what we think."

—BUDDHA

"Change your thoughts and you change your world."

—NORMAN VINCENT PEALE

"You are today where your thoughts have brought you; you will be to-morrow where your thoughts take you."

—JAMES ALLEN

"We become what we think about."

—EARL NIGHTINGALE

"The highest possible stage in moral culture is when we recognize that we ought to control our thoughts."

—CHARLES DARWIN

"Why are we Masters of our fate, the captains of our souls? Because we have the power to control our thoughts."

—ALFRED A. MONTAPERT

Our words indicate what we are thinking and our thoughts create our lives. People fall along a great continuum of being positive or negative. In my experience, I have never known anyone who thinks they are a negative person. No one I've yet known truly gets it when their thoughts are more destructive than constructive. Their words may reveal this to others, but they don't hear it. They may complain constantly—I was one of them—but most people, myself included, think they are a positive, upbeat, optimistic, and sanguine person.

It is vital that we control our minds in order to re-create our lives. The purple Complaint Free bracelets help us realize exactly where we are on the continuum of positive and negative expression. And then, when we go through the repeated practice of moving the bracelet from wrist to wrist, over and over, time after time, we truly begin to notice our words. In so doing, we begin to notice our thoughts. When we notice our thoughts, we can change and ultimately reshape our lives into whatever we choose. The purple bracelets help us set a trap for our own negativity so it can be caught and then released, never to return.

That Sunday back in July 2006, after handing out the very first no-complaint purple bracelets to my congregation and inviting everyone to commit to trying to go 21 consecutive days complaint free, I shared a story:

"When I was a boy," I said, "I used to stand by the lake and throw rocks as far as I could out into the water. After the initial splash, I would watch as the ripples from the impact traveled out in every direction until they lapped the shores of the cove on every side. Together, we can create a ripple; right here, right now, in this small community, we can begin something that can touch and transform the world."

Their tentative energy began to shift to enthusiasm.

"Let's give these purple bracelets free to anyone who asks for them," I said. "Together, we'll make Kansas City, Missouri, the first 'Complaint Free' city in the United States!" Then I added, "Considering the way the Royals have played baseball this year, we've got a long road ahead of us."

The room fell silent. Realizing my complaint, I moved my bracelet from my right wrist to my left for the first time—but certainly not the last.

People from our community began to hear about the purple bracelets. We ordered another 500, and they were committed before they arrived. We thought about ordering another thousand but wondered what we'd do with the leftover bracelets. We ordered them, and before the thousand came in they, too, were spoken for. Requests trickled in for them. The trickle became a drizzle, a downpour, and then a deluge.

Sensing something important was unfolding, I called *The Kansas City Star* to ask who at the paper might be interested in a story like this. They referred me to Helen Gray, so I sent her an e-mail explaining what was happening.

As we sent the bracelets out, I found out personally how difficult this transformation could be. The first day, my hands got tired switching the bracelet from wrist to wrist. I realized that I was complaining all the time. I wanted to call it quits, but everyone at church was watching me. After the first week, my personal best was to have only switched the bracelet five times in one day. And yet the following day, I was back up to twelve times, but I kept at it. I never thought of myself as a person who complained, but I was finding out otherwise. As I was struggling with not complaining, criticizing, or gossiping, I was simultaneously discouraged and glad that I'd not heard back from Ms. Gray at *The Star*. Although I thought this was a good idea, I certainly didn't feel as if I was excelling at the experiment and did not want to have to tell the reporter, "Yes, I'm the minister who challenged everyone to do this." And "Me? Well, after two weeks of really trying, I've made it almost six hours."

I stayed with it. Finally, after nearly a month, I had a string of three days going. Every Sunday, my congregation would look to see which arm the bracelet was on. I could see that some of them had taken off their bracelets. But many were staying with it. This inspired me tremendously. Finally, I wrote down a goal to "go 21 consecutive days complaint free by September 31." I read this goal three times each morning and three times each night. Slowly, I began to make progress.

I found that I could do very well around some people but not so well around others. Sadly, I realized that my relationships with some people I considered good friends centered on expressing our dissatisfaction about whatever we were talking about. I began to avoid them. I felt guilty at first, but I noticed that my bracelet stayed put. More important, I found myself beginning to feel happier.

After more than a month, Ms. Gray from *The Kansas City Star* e-mailed to say she'd been on vacation. She said she found the idea intriguing and wanted to write a story about our Complaint Free bracelets. As she was preparing the article, I finally completed my 21 days. When her first story came out, I was the only person to have made it.

I again confirmed with my church board that we would give bracelets free to anyone who wanted them. "We can help raise the consciousness of the world," we agreed. Little did we know that other papers would pick up the story from *The Kansas City Star.* Within weeks, we had requests for nearly 9,000 purple bracelets. We bought every purple bracelet our supplier had and ordered more. Volunteers stepped forward to automate our Web site so that bracelet requests would be taken directly from it, generating labels that our fulfillment team would use to package them. We acquired the Web site address TheComplaintFreeChurch.org and more newspapers picked up the story, followed by television stations.

The idea was becoming bigger than just our church in Kansas City. A Catholic diocese requested 2,000 purple bracelets for everyone in their churches and schools. We started getting requests from places like Australia, Belgium, and South Africa. This was becoming a genuine worldwide phenomenon. Sensing that our "ripple in a pond" idea was actually going to make it around the planet, we purchased the Web site address AComplaint FreeWorld.org.

In time, we created a data-entry team, a fulfillment team, a supplies team, and a shipping team, all staffed by volunteers.

After 100-plus newspaper stories, *The Today Show,* and a true national launch on *The Oprah Winfrey Show,* our movement is now millions strong and growing rapidly around the world! When I was interviewed by an associate producer for *The Oprah Winfrey Show,* I was asked what my goal was for this campaign. "To transform the consciousness of our world," I said. She looked at me and smiled sympathetically, "That's a pretty big dream, don't you think?" I returned her smile and said, "Do the math."

As I write this, we've received requests for nearly 6 million purple bracelets from people in more than 80 countries and we're receiving requests for approximately 1,000 bracelets every day. The average person takes 4 to 8 months to successfully make 21 days. Multiply the number of bracelets by the number of times most people complain and the world is already awakening to a new consciousness.

How many complaints have already been quelled as a result of this simple idea? How much more positive are homes, schools, workplaces, churches, sports teams, hospitals, prisons, police departments, fire departments, clinics, the military, and government agencies now as compared to just a handful of months ago? In every corner of our world, there are people in all of these groups who are wearing purple bracelets and striving assiduously to frame their words only in the positive.

Transform the world? It's happening.

There are two things upon which most people will agree:

1. There is too much complaining in the world.
2. The state of the world is not the way we would like it.

In my opinion, there is a correlation between the two. We are focusing on what is wrong rather than focusing our vision on a healthy, happy, and harmonious world. And you are now part of this. It's no accident that you have picked up this book. You have answered your soul's call to stop being part of the problem and to become part of the solution. You can change the world by simply becoming an example of positive change. You can bear the torch for a bright future for our children by taking this challenge and staying with it, however long it takes, until you succeed. You can be a healing cell in the body of humanity.

The other day, I was at a Kansas City Royals game and there was a group of fans trying desperately to get a "wave" going around the stadium. The wave would begin with great enthusiasm as people leapt to their feet, raising their arms, and letting out a big "whoop!" It traveled around the park but began to fade at a certain section. The fans in that section, for whatever reason, were not committed to the wave and it stopped; the wave died.

This wave of human-consciousness transformation has now been passed on to you. You can keep it going. You can help create a Complaint Free World. Do it for those around you. Do it for your nation. Do it because it's a powerful first step toward world peace. Do it for your children and their children yet to come. But mostly, do it for yourself.

Do this for myself? Isn't that selfish? No. There is nothing wrong with doing something so you will benefit. As you become a happier person, you raise the overall level of happiness in the world. You will send out a vibration of optimism and hope that will resound with others of similar intent. You will create a network of expectation for a brighter future for all.

Anthropologist Margaret Mead once wrote that we should "never doubt that a small group of thoughtful, committed citizens can change the world. Indeed, it is the only thing that ever has."

The ripple continues.

Oh, and P.S.: Marcia made it!

PART I

Unconscious
Incompetence

I Complain Therefore I Am

Man invented language to satisfy his deep need
to complain.

—LILY TOMLIN

Complain: (verb) 1: to express grief, pain, or
discontent <complaining about the weather>
2: to make a formal accusation or charge

—THE MERRIAM-WEBSTER DICTIONARY

There are four stages to become competent at anything. In becoming a Complaint Free person, you
will go through each of them and, sorry, you can't skip
steps. You can't jump over them and effect lasting change.
Some of the stages last longer than others. Everyone's experience with them varies. You might soar through one
stage and then become stuck in another for a long time,
but if you stay with it you will master this skill.

VOICES

Like most of the other folks who took up the Complaint free challenge, I quickly discovered exactly how many of the words I spoke in daily interactions were complaints. For the first time, I really heard myself when I vented about work, whined about my aches and pains, bemoaned political and world issues, and complained about the weather. What a shock to realize how many of my words held negative energy—and I considered myself such a positive person!

—MARTY POINTER, KANSAS CITY, MO

The four stages to competency are:

1. Unconscious Incompetence
2. Conscious Incompetence
3. Conscious Competence
4. Unconscious Competence

In "On a Distant Prospect of Eton College," Thomas Gray gave us the saying "ignorance is bliss." As you become a Complaint Free person, you begin in the bliss of ignorance, move through the turmoil of transformation, and arrive at true bliss. Right now, you are in the Unconscious Incompetence stage. You are unconscious about your being incompetent. You don't realize (are unconscious) as to how much you complain (are incompetent).

Unconscious Incompetence is as much a state of being as a stage of competency. This is where we all begin. In

Unconscious Incompetence you are pure potential, ready to create great things for yourself. There are exciting new vistas about to be explored. All you have to do is be willing to go through the remaining steps.

Many people are an "ouch!" looking for a hurt. If you cry "ouch," the hurt will show up. If you complain, you'll receive more to complain about. It's the Law of Attraction in action. As you complete these stages, as you leave complaining behind, as you are no longer an "ouch" looking for a hurt, your life will unfold for you like a beautiful spring flower.

One of the questions I'm often asked is "Can I never complain . . . ever!?" To which I answer, "Of course you can complain." I say this for two reasons:

1. I'm not out to tell you or anyone else what to do. If I were, I'd be trying to change you, and that means I'm focusing on something about you I don't like. I'd be expressing discontent about you and, by inference, complaining. So you can do whatever you want. It's your choice.
2. Sometimes it makes sense to complain.

Now, before you feel you've found your loophole in number 2 above, consider that word "sometimes" and remember that I and many, many people have gone three consecutive weeks—that's 21 days, or 504 hours in a row—without complaining at all. No complaints, zero, zip! When it comes to complaining, "sometimes" means "not very often at all." Complaining should happen infrequently; criticism and gossip, never. If we are honest with ourselves, life events that lead us to legitimately complain (express grief, pain, or discontent) are exceedingly rare. Most of the complaining we do is just a lot of "ear pollution" detrimental to our happiness and well-being.

Check yourself. When you complain (express grief, pain, or discontent), is the cause severe? Are you complaining frequently? Has it been a month or more since you complained? If you're complaining more than once a month, you might just be giving in to habitual griping, which doesn't serve you. You're an "ouch" looking for a hurt.

To be a happy person who has mastered your thoughts and has begun creating your life by design, you need a very, very high threshold of what leads you to express grief, pain, and discontent. The next time you're about to complain about something, ask yourself how the situation stacks up to something that happened to me a few years ago.

I was sitting in my office preparing a lesson. The home we lived in at the time was located at a sharp bend in the road. Drivers had to slow down to make the curve, and just 200 yards past our house the city road became a county highway and the speed limit changed from 25 mph to 55 mph. As a result, we lived on an acceleration/deceleration lane. If it weren't for the curve in the road, our home would have been in a very dangerous place.

It was a warm spring afternoon and the lace curtains flapped softly in the breeze from the open windows. Suddenly, I heard a strange sound. There was a loud thud, followed by a scream. It wasn't the scream of a person, but rather that of an animal. Every animal, just like every person, has a unique voice, and I knew this voice well. It was our long-haired golden retriever, Ginger. Normally, we don't think of dogs screaming. Barking, howling, whimpering—yes; but screaming is something we rarely hear. But that's exactly what Ginger was doing. She had been hit, and she lay in the road shrieking with pain not twenty feet outside my window. I shouted and ran through the living room and out the front door, followed by my wife, Gail, and my daughter, Lia. Lia was six at the time.

As we approached Ginger, we could tell she was badly hurt. She was using her front legs to try to stand, but her hind legs did not seem to be helping. Again and again she yowled in pain. Neighbors poured from their homes to see what was causing the commotion. Lia just kept saying her name, "Ginger . . . Ginger . . . ," as the tears flowed down her cheeks and wet her shirt.

I looked around for the driver who had hit Ginger but saw no one. Then I looked up the hill that marked the line between city road and county road and saw a truck, towing a trailer, cresting the hill and accelerating past 55 mph. Even though our dog lay there in agony, my wife stood in shock, and my daughter cried piteously, I was consumed with confronting the person who had hit

Ginger. "How could anyone do this and just drive off?!" I thought. "He was just coming around the curve . . . surely he saw her, surely he knew what happened!"

Abandoning my family in the midst of their pain and confusion, I jumped into my car and spun out of the driveway, leaving a plume of dust and gravel. Sixty, 75, 83 miles per hour along the gravel-and-dirt road in pursuit of the person who had hit Lia's dog and left without so much as facing us. I was going so fast on the uncertain surface that my car began to feel as if it were floating tenuously above the ground. In that moment, I calmed myself enough to realize that if I were killed while driving, it would be even harder on Gail and Lia than Ginger's having been hurt. I slowed down just enough to control my car as the distance between me and other driver closed.

Turning into his driveway and still not realizing I was after him, the man stepped from his truck in a torn shirt and oily jeans. I skidded in behind him and jumped from my car, screaming, "You hit my dog!!!" The man turned and looked at me as if I were speaking a foreign language. With blood raging in my ears, I wasn't sure I heard him correctly when he said, "I know I hit your dog. . . . What are you going to do about it?" After regaining my connection with reality, I shot back, "WHAT?!? What did you say?!" He smiled as if he were correcting an errant child and then said again, in slow, deliberate words, "I know I hit your dog. . . . Exactly what are you going to do about it?"

I was blind with rage. In my mind I kept seeing Lia in my rearview mirror standing over Ginger and crying. "Put up your hands," I yelled. "What?" he said. "Put up your hands," I said again. "Defend yourself . . . I'm going to kill you!"

A few moments before, reason had kept me from killing myself while driving in a white-hot rage to find this guy. Now his dismissive and cavalier comment about having painfully wounded a pet I dearly loved had vanquished all reason. I had never been in a fight in my adult life. I didn't believe in fighting. I wasn't sure I knew how to fight. But I wanted to beat this man to death. In that moment, I didn't care if I ended up in prison.

"I ain't gonna fight you," he said. "And if you hit me, it's assault, mister." My arms raised, my fists clinched tight as diamonds, I stood there dumbfounded. "Fight me!" I said. "No, sir," he said, smiling through his remaining teeth, "I ain't gonna do no such thing." He turned his back and slowly walked away. I stood there shaking, anger poisoning my blood.

I don't remember driving back to my family. I don't remember lifting Ginger up and taking her to the vet. I do remember the way she smelled the last time I held her and the way she whimpered softly as the vet's needle ended her suffering. "How could a person do such a thing?" I asked myself repeatedly.

Days later, the man's jagged smile still haunted me as I tried to sleep. His "What are you going to do about it?"

rang in my ears. I visualized exactly what I would have done to him had we fought. In my visions I was a super-hero destroying an evil villain. Sometimes, I imagined I had a baseball bat or other weapon and was hurting him, hurting him as badly as he had hurt me, my wife, my daughter, and Ginger.

On the third night of unsuccessful attempts to sleep, I got up and began to write in my journal. After spilling out my grief, pain, and discontent for nearly an hour, I wrote something surprising: "Those who hurt are hurt-ing." Taking in my words as if they were from someone else, I wondered aloud, "What?" Again I wrote, "Those who hurt are hurting." I sat back, brooding in my chair, and listened to the spring peepers and the crickets cele-brating the night. "Those who hurt are hurting? How could that apply to this guy?"

As I thought more about it, I began to understand. A person who could so easily hurt a treasured family pet must not know the love of companion animals as we do. A person who can drive away as a young child folds into tears could not know the love of a young child. A man who cannot apologize for spearing a family's heart must have had his heart speared many, many times. This man was the real victim in this story. Truly he had acted as a villain, but it came as a result of the depth of pain within him.

I sat a long time, letting this all sink in. Every time I began to feel angry at him and the pain he caused, I thought of the pain this man must live with on a daily basis. In time, I switched off the light, went to bed, and slept soundly.

Complain: to express grief, pain, or discontent.

During this experience, I felt **grief**. Ginger had shown up five years ago at our home in rural South Carolina. Several dogs had come to our home wanting to stay, but Gibson, our other dog, always ran them off. For some reason, he let Ginger stay. There was something special about Ginger. We presumed from her demeanor that she had been abused prior to coming to us. And, because she especially shied away from me, it was probably a man who had hurt her. After a year or so, she had begun to tentatively trust me. And in the remaining years, she had become a true friend. I deeply grieved her passing.

I certainly felt **pain**, real emotional pain that tore at my soul. Those of us with children know that we would rather endure any pain than have our children do so. And the pain my Lia was going through redoubled my own.

I felt **discontent**. I felt torn for not having thrashed the guy as well as for having considered acting violently in the first place. I felt ashamed for having walked away from him and equally ashamed for having chased after him in the first place.

Grief. Pain. Discontent.

When this man hit Ginger, it was appropriate for me to have felt and to have expressed each of these. You may have experienced something equally difficult at some time in your life. Fortunately, such traumatic events are rare. Similarly, complaining (expressing grief, pain, or discontent) should be rare.

But for most of us, our complaints are not sourced by such deeply painful experiences. Rather, we're the character in the Joe Walsh song "Life's Been Good"—we can't complain, but sometimes we still do. Things are not really bad enough to warrant expressing grief, pain, or discontent, but complaining is our default setting. It's what we do.

Ignorance is bliss. Prior to beginning your trek down the path to becoming a Complaint Free person, you were probably blissfully unaware as to how much you complain and the damaging effect of your complaints on your life. For many of us, griping about the weather, our spouse, our work, our bodies, our friends, our jobs, the economy, other drivers, our country, or whatever we are thinking about is something we do dozens of times each and every day. Yet few of us realize how often we complain.

The words come out of our mouths, so our ears must hear them. But, for some reason, they don't register as complaints. Complaining can be likened to bad breath. We notice it when it comes out of someone else's mouth, but not when it comes from our own.

Chances are you complain a lot more than you think. And now that you've accepted the 21-day challenge to become complaint free, you have begun to notice it. You start moving the bracelet from wrist to wrist, and you realize how much you kvetch (Yiddish for "complain"—I'm not Jewish, but I really like the word).

Up until this point, you would probably have said, honestly, that you don't complain—much, anyway. Certainly, you think that you only complain when something is legitimately bothering you. The next time you're tempted to justify your complaining, remember Ginger's story and ask yourself if what you're going through is that bad. Then resolve to keep your pledge to not complain.

Everyone who has become a 21-Day Complaint Free Champion has said to me, "It wasn't easy, but it was worth it." Nothing valuable is ever easy. Simple? Yes. But "easy" is not part of becoming a successful person. I say this not to scare you but to inspire you. If you find becoming a Complaint Free person (monitoring and changing your words) difficult, it doesn't mean that you can't do it. And it doesn't mean there is something wrong with you. M. H. Alderson said, "If at first you don't succeed, you're running about average." If you're complaining, you're right where you're supposed to be. Now you're becoming aware of it, and you can begin to erase it from your life.

You can do this. I complained dozens of times every single day, and I made it. The key is to not give up. There is a wonderful woman in my church who is still wearing one of the original purple bracelets we gave out. Hers is now tattered and gray, but she told me recently, "They might bury me with this thing, but I'm not giving up."

That's the level of commitment it takes. The good news is that even before you make 21 consecutive days of not complaining, you will find your internal focus shifting and yourself becoming happier. Here is an e-mail I received today:

Hi,
Like thousands, I have already begun changing my focus. While waiting for my bracelet, I have started to wear a rubber band around my wrist. This has made me aware of what I'm doing. I've been doing this for about a week, and I am now rarely complaining. *The remarkable thing about this is how much happier I feel!* Not to mention how much happier those around me must be (like my husband!). I have wanted to work on my complaining for a long time and the bracelet campaign has been the impetus for my changing behavior.

The subject of the bracelets and the mission behind them has come up in MANY conversations, so the mission has a HUGE ripple effect where MANY people are at least thinking about how often they complain and perhaps deciding to behave differently. This movement may have a very far reaching effect as more and more people hear of the idea. The reach of this mission is far greater than those who actually get the bracelets! Awesome to think about!

Jeanne Reilly
Rockville, Md.

Venerated radio commentator Paul Harvey once said, "I hope one day to achieve enough of what the world calls success so that if someone asks me how I did it I will tell them, 'I get up more times than I fall.'" As with all things worth accomplishing, you must fail your way to success. If you're like most when you begin this process, you will probably move your bracelet from arm to arm until you get sore and tired of doing it. I moved my bracelet so many times that I broke three of them before making it 21 consecutive days. If you break yours, go to www.AComplaintFreeWorld.org and ask for another.

But if you'll stay with it, one day you'll be lying in bed about to drift off to sleep and glance at your wrist. There, for the first time in days, months, or even years, you'll see that your purple bracelet is on the same wrist as it was when you got out of bed that morning. You'll think, "I must have complained at some point today and just not caught myself." But as you do a mental inventory, you'll realize that you made it. You actually made it one whole day without complaining! One day at a time. You can do it.

As you begin this transformation, you are fortunate, because even with my warnings of the difficulty ahead, you have a psychological advantage working for you. It's called the Dunning-Kruger effect. Whenever a person tries something new, whether it be snow skiing, juggling, playing the flute, riding a horse, meditating, writing a book, painting a picture, or anything, it is part of human nature to think it will be simple to master. The Dunning-

Kruger effect is named for Justin Kruger and David Dunning of Cornell University, who did studies on people attempting to learn new skills. Their results, published in the *Journal of Personality and Social Psychology* in December 1999, stated that "ignorance more frequently begets confidence than does knowledge." In other words, you're not aware that doing something is difficult, so you try it. You think, "This is going to be easy," so you begin, and getting started is the most difficult part.

Without the Dunning-Kruger effect, if we knew the amount of effort it would actually take to become proficient at a new skill, we would probably give up before we begin. My wife, Gail, sums it up well. When asked, "What's the best way to learn to ride a horse?" Gail always responds, "Time in the saddle . . . time in the saddle."

Time in the saddle. Wearing the purple bracelet (or rubber band, coin in your pocket, or other self-monitoring tool) and moving it. Moving it every time you complain. Moving it even though it seems hard, embarrassing, or frustrating. Moving it even after you've made it ten days. Starting over again and again. Staying with it even if others around you have given up. Staying with it even if others around you have succeeded and your personal best so far is two days. Staying with it . . . time in the saddle . . . time in the saddle.

There is an old story of two construction workers sitting down to eat lunch together. One opens his lunch box and complains, "Yech! A meatloaf sandwich . . . I hate meatloaf sandwiches." His friend says nothing. The following day, the two meet up again for lunch. Again the first worker opens his lunch box, looks inside, and, this time more agitated, says, "Another meatloaf sandwich!? I'm sick and tired of meatloaf sandwiches. I hate meatloaf sandwiches!" As before, his colleague remains silent. The third day, the two are preparing to eat lunch when the first construction worker opens his lunch box and begins to shout, "I've had it!! Day in and day out it's the same thing! Meatloaf sandwiches every blessed day! I want something else!" Wanting to be helpful, his friend asks, "Why don't you just ask your wife to make you something else?" With bewilderment on his face, the first man replies, "What are you talking about? I make my own lunch."

Tired of meatloaf sandwiches? You're making your own lunch each and every day. Change what you are saying. Stop complaining. Change your words, change your thoughts, and you will change your life. When Jesus said, "Seek and ye shall find," it was a statement of universal principle. What you seek, you will find. When you complain, you are using the incredible power of your mind to seek things that you say you don't want but nonetheless draw them to you. Then you complain about these new things and attract more of what you don't want. You get caught in the "complaint loop"—a self-fulfilling prophecy of complaint: manifestation, complaint: manifestation, complaint: manifestation, and on and on it goes.

In *The Outsider*, Albert Camus wrote, "Gazing up at the dark sky spangled with its signs and stars, for the first time, I laid my heart open to the benign indifference of the universe." The Universe is benign indifference. The Universe, or God, or Spirit, or whatever you choose to call it, is benign (good), but it is also indifferent (it does not care). The Universe doesn't care if you use the power of your thoughts as indicated by your words to call to yourself love, health, happiness, abundance, and peace, or if you attract to yourself pain, suffering, misery, loneliness, and poverty. Our thoughts create our world, our words indicate our thoughts. When we control our words by eradicating complaining, we create our lives with intention and attract what we desire.

CHAPTER 2

Complaining and Health

Of all the self-fulfilling prophecies in our
culture, the assumption that aging means decline
and poor health is probably the deadliest.
—MARILYN FERGUSON,
THE AQUARIAN CONSPIRACY

We complain for the same reason we do anything:
We perceive a benefit from doing so. I remember
vividly the night I discovered the benefits of complaining.
I was thirteen years old and at a sock hop. If you're too
young to remember, sock hops were dances, often held at
high school gyms. They were called sock hops because
the kids attending were required to remove their shoes to
protect the gymnasium floors. These dances were popular
in the United States during the 1950s, but a resurgence of

I came home from work early yesterday and having had an exceptionally tough day with my back (major spinal fusion/ cervical fusions), I just wanted to relax and feel sorry for myself. At 47, I have a laundry list of medical issues that weigh me down. But when I plopped on the couch and watched you on *Oprah*, I was inspired!

I complain eve ry day about my pain and am on so many pain medications. You are right, the complaints do weigh me down, and I want to participate in the no complaint zone. I have ordered 10 bracelets for myself, and some friends. I will be sending a small donation at a later time for these bracelets, but mostly am writing to you to say thank you.

I am most grateful to God that I CAN walk; I have good friends, a loving family, and a good job. I need to re-focus my energies on being grateful and not wallow in self-pity for my myriad of medical problems. Thank you from the bottom of my heart.

—CINDY LAFOLLETT, CAMBRIDGE, OH

sock hops occurred with the 1973 release of George Lucas's film *American Graffti*. In 1973, the church I attended sponsored a sock hop for teenagers. Being thirteen at the time, and thereby a teenager, I went to the dance.

Being a thirteen-year-old boy is interesting, to say the least. For the first time, girls are no longer "gross." When you're a thirteen-year-old boy, girls are both magnetically alluring and, simultaneously, terrifying. Terrifying as they might be, when I was thirteen girls occupied my every waking thought and haunted my dreams. Thoughts of skateboards, model ships, movies, and comics were all swept from my consciousness by thoughts of girls. I was under their spell. I wanted desperately to connect with girls but had no idea how to do so or what I'd do once I did. I was like the old joke about a dog chasing cars that finally caught one and then didn't know what to do with it. I wanted to be close to girls but was afraid to come near them.

The night of the sock hop was hot and humid. The girls were adorned in poodle skirts, bouffant hairdos, saddle shoes, and bright red lipstick. The boys' costumes consisted primarily of peg-leg jeans rolled up at the ankles, a white T-shirt with a cigarette pack (borrowed from our parents) rolled up in the sleeve, penny loafers with pennies in them, and hair slicked back into a style called a DA. The soundtrack from *American Graffiti* played over and over again as the girls stood giggling on one side of the room and I and the other boys kept to the opposite side of the room, lounging on metal folding chairs and desperately trying to look cool. We were panic-stricken about going over to the girls, even though every strand of our DNA begged us to do so. If we looked cool enough, we reasoned, perhaps the girls would come to us. If not, at least they would think we didn't care if they did or not.

My best friend at the time, Chip, was tall, a good student, and a great athlete. Of the three, I was, well, tall.

And unlike Chip, I was quite chubby. For as long as I could remember, clothes shopping meant my mother and me taking the escalator to the basement of Belk's Department Store. The basement was the home of the "husky" (fat boys') department and the only place I could find clothes that fit.

Because Chip was in such good shape, I could tell that several of the girls were eyeing him. It hurt to know that he was more attractive to them than I was, and it also bothered me that Chip just sat there with us rather than going over and talking to one of them.

"I'm too shy," Chip said. "I don't know what to say." "Just go over there; let them do the talking," I said. "You can't just sit here all night." "YOU'RE just sitting here," Chip said, "and you're Mr. Talkative. You go over and say something to them."

Drug addicts will often remember the first time they tried what would ultimately become their "drug of choice," the drug that would consume and possibly take their lives if they couldn't shake their addiction to it. With my next sentence, I was about to embark on an addiction to complaining that would last more than thirty years. I looked at Chip and said, "Even if I went over there and talked to them, they wouldn't dance with me. I'm too fat. Look at me, I'm thirteen and I shot past 200 pounds a long time ago. I wheeze when I talk. I sweat when I walk—I'd probably fall down if I danced. You're in great shape. The girls are looking at you." The other guys nodded in agreement. "I'm just a funny guy they like to talk to about the boys they do like. I'm too fat. They don't want me . . . and they never will."

At that moment, another good friend walked up from behind and slapped me on the back. "Hey, fat boy!" he said. Normally, his greeting would have meant nothing. Nearly everyone called me "fat boy." It was a nickname I'd grown used to. I never took it as an insult. These were my friends and it didn't matter to them that I was fat. But when I was called "fat boy" after having just given a greatly embellished speech on how tough it was being overweight as a way of getting myself out of going over to the girls, the effect in our little circle was palpable. One of my other friends said, "Hey, shut up!" "Leave him alone!" another said. "It's not his fault he's fat!" a third said. Every one of them looked at me with great concern.

"Play it up!" my mind said. So I sighed and looked away dramatically. When I complained about my body and its probable impact on my chances with the girls, I had gotten the other guys' attention, their sympathy, and I had gotten myself off the hook from going over and talking to the young ladies. My drug had kicked in. I had found my addiction. Complaining could get me high.

Years later, when I didn't get a job, I told myself and others it was because I was fat. When I got a traffic ticket, it was because I was fat. It would take me another five and a half years to shed this excuse and the weight that was damaging my health.

Psychologist Robin Kowalski wrote that many complaints "involve attempts to elicit particular interpersonal reactions from others, such as sympathy or approval. For example, people may complain about their health, not because they actually feel sick but because the *sick role* allows them to achieve secondary gains such as sympathy from others or the avoidance of aversive events."*

By complaining and playing the "fat card," I had gotten sympathy and approval, and I had a justifiable reason for not talking to the girls. My complaining had benefited me. You may have done something similar at some point in your life. We complain to get sympathy, attention, and to avoid stepping up to something we're afraid of doing. When I was a kid and had symptoms of the flu or other illness, I'd play it up to stay home from school and watch TV. The odd thing was, I'd often find myself getting sicker after complaining about how I felt.

Have you ever played the sick role? Are you doing so now? Poor health is one of the most common complaints people voice. People complain about their health to get sympathy and attention and to avoid "aversive events" such as adopting a healthier lifestyle. When we complain about our health, we may receive these benefits, but at what cost?

*Kowalski, R. M. (1996). Complaints and complaining: Functions, antecedents, and consequences. *Psychological Bulletin* 119, page 180.

You have probably heard the term "psychosomatic illness." A psychosomatic illness is caused by the mental processes of the sufferer rather than physiological causes. There is a tendency in our society to believe that psychosomatic illnesses are "made up" by a small number of disturbed individuals. Many believe that these diseases, having been created by the patient, are not to be taken seriously. However, doctors estimate that nearly two-thirds of their time is spent treating patients whose illnesses have psychological origins.*

Think about that. Two-thirds of illnesses originate in the mind. Indeed, the word *psychosomatic* comes from *psyche,* meaning "mind," and *soma,* meaning "body." Therefore, psychosomatic literally means "mind/body." There is a connection between the mind and the body. What the mind believes, the body manifests. Dozens of research studies have shown that what a person believes about their health leads to that belief becoming real for them. I heard a story on National Public Radio where doctors found that if they told patients a drug held great promise in curing them, the drug had a far greater beneficial effect than it did for patients who received the same drug without such a suggestion. The story went on to report one study that found that Alzheimer's patients who had other physical illnesses, such as high blood pressure, did not get the full benefit of the drugs they took because,

*Ibid., page 186.

due to their diminished memory, they could not remember taking their daily medications. The mind has a powerful effect on the body.

A few months ago, I was called to the hospital to be with a longtime member of my church. Before I entered her room, I stopped as I normally do at the nurses' station to ask the doctors and nurses about her prognosis. "She's fine," said one nurse. Her doctor added, "She's had a stroke, but she'll recover fully." Entering her room, I saw someone who looked anything but "fine." "Jane," I said. "Hello, Jane, it's me—Reverend Will." "Reverend Will," she said faintly, "I'm so glad you came. I've only got a few days. . . . I'm dying."

"You're what?" I asked. "I'm dying," she said. At that moment, a nurse came in to check her vitals and I pulled her aside. "I thought you said she was okay," I said to the nurse. "She is," the nurse said. "But Jane just told me she's dying," I said. Rolling her eyes in exasperation, the nurse walked over to the bed. "Jane? Jane!" Jane opened her eyes. "You've had a stroke, hon', you're not dying. You're going to be okay. Just a few days and then we'll move you into rehab. You'll be home with your cat, Marty, in no time, okay?" "Okay," Jane said, smiling.

Jane waited until the nurse left the room and then began to give me details for her upcoming funeral. "But you're not dying!" I protested. "I'll make notes, and when you die—a long time from now—then I can do your funeral." Jane shook her head. "I'm dying now," she said, and she went on to give me the particulars of her memorial service.

On my way out, I talked to the doctor again. "She's convinced she's dying," I said. She smiled, "Look, we're all going to die someday, even Jane. But she's only had a stroke, and it's not going to kill her. She's really going to be okay."

Two weeks later, I officiated at Jane's funeral. The doctors and nurses could not convince her she was not going to die. She had convinced herself she was dying and her body believed her.

When you complain about your health, you are putting out negative statements that your body hears. It registers and your mind (*psyche*) directs the energy in your body (*soma*), attracting more health challenges. Have you ever noticed that the people who complain about their health invariably have more and more to complain about?

"But I really am sick," you say. Please understand that I don't doubt you believe you are. But remember that doctors estimate that 67 percent of illnesses are a result of "thinking sick." Our thoughts create our world and our words indicate our thoughts. Complaining about an illness will neither shorten its duration nor lessen its severity.

I invite you to consider how much your talking about your sickness might be an attempt to get sympathy and attention. You may not want to answer that question, but it's an important one to at least entertain. When you complain about your health, remember that you might be trying to put out a fire with gasoline. You might want to get healthy, but when you complain about your illness you are sending health-limiting waves of energy throughout your body.

In 1999, at the age of thirty-nine, a good friend of mine named Hal was diagnosed with stage IV lung cancer. The doctors estimated he would die in less than six months. In addition to this mortal diagnosis, Hal was also facing other challenges. Even though he had made his living selling health insurance, he had none. His bills piled up and it was a constant struggle to keep the lights on and his family fed. When I found out he was dying, I visited Hal and was astounded by his upbeat attitude. He didn't complain but talked about how great his life had been and how fortunate he was.

Through it all, Hal kept his great sense of humor. One day I invited him to take a walk, but because he was so weak we never made it out of the front yard. We stood in front of his home enjoying the fresh air and talked. As we did, Hal noticed several large buzzards making slow, lazy circles directly over where he stood. Hal pointed to the buzzards and said, "Oooh, a bad sign!" When I saw the devilish glint in his eye, we both exploded into laughter.

When our laughter subsided, I asked, "How do you manage to not complain with all you're going through?" Hal leaned on his cane and said, "Easy, it's not the fifteenth." Feeling he'd adequately answered my question, Hal began to walk slowly back to the house. "What the heck does the fifteenth have to do with anything?" I asked. He said, "When I was diagnosed, I knew it was going to be tough and that I could go through it cursing God, science, and everyone else. Or I could focus on the good things in my life. So I decided to give myself one unhappy day each month to complain. I randomly picked the fifteenth. Whenever anything happens that I might want to complain about, I tell myself that I have to wait until the fifteenth." "Does that work?" I asked. "Pretty well," he said. "But don't you get really down on the fifteenth of each month?" I asked. "No," he replied. "By the time the fifteenth gets here, I've forgotten what it was I was going to complain about."

Even though we lived more than two hours apart, I visited Hal twice a week until he made his life's transition. People would tell me what a great friend I was and how thoughtful I was to devote so much time to him. The truth is that I did it for me. Hal taught me that even in the midst of something as challenging as a terminal illness, one can find happiness. Oh, and he didn't die within six months. He lived more than two happy years blessing those around him. I miss him, but the positive imprint he made in my life is indelible. And he beat the odds by a factor of four. That's the health-affirming power of living a life of gratitude rather than one of complaint.

By this time in our journey, you've begun to get glimpses into your complaining. You've begun to become conscious of your incompetence. You are noticing when you complain. You are into Conscious Incompetence.

PART 2

Conscious
Incompetence

CHAPTER 3

Complaining and Relationships

It is a waste of time to be angry about my
disability. One has to get on with life and I
haven't done badly. People won't have time for
you if you are always angry or complaining.

—STEPHEN HAWKING

When you enter the Conscious Incompetence stage,
you are uncomfortably aware (conscious) of just
how often you complain (are incompetent).

When we complain, we may gain the benefits of attention or sympathy. We may also avoid having to do
something that causes us to stretch. But we walk a fine
line when we complain. Chronic complainers can end up
ostracized by those around them who find their energy
drained by the complainer. You probably know people

VOICES

I first learned of this wonderful program on *The Today Show.*
I began asking my coworkers if they would be interested in
doing this. The majority of them agreed and we ordered our
bracelets. We decided that while we were waiting for them
to arrive, we would set one day of our business week aside
and try not to complain on that given day. We now set
Mondays aside as NO MOAN MONDAYS.

We have signs posted on our company bulletin board
and around the office to remind employees to try not to
moan, gripe, or complain on Mondays. It really has been an
inspiration in our office and we usually greet each other on
Mondays with "Welcome to No Moan Monday!"

When you think about it, life is just too short. We are
always looking for those big blessings in life (i.e., more
money, job security, weight loss, etc.), but we need to start
looking for those tiny blessings that are given to us each day.
I think this program is wonderful. We are so blessed!

—SALLY SCUDIERE, KENT, OH

who leave you feeling depleted. Through their complaining nature, these people literally draw your energy as it is
converted into commiseration. Conversely, people in seri-
ous situations can remain upbeat and not allow themselves to feel like a victim. Even though he was dying, I
never felt drained by my friend Hal. Rather, I was buoyed
by his optimism and cheerfulness.

People tend to run along a continuum in degrees of
rarely complaining to constantly complaining. If a person

within a group falls too far out of the norm for the group, in time that person will find that he or she is no longer welcome.

Again, to look at complaining as a drug, many of us have been in situations where others were drinking excessively, smoking, or doing drugs. If someone didn't go along with the group, the individuals in the group felt threatened. My personal theory regarding this phenomenon is that the individuals practicing the destructive behaviors know they are not making healthy choices and feel this magnified in comparison to the person who is not imbibing. When we're around others who complain more or less than us, it feels uncomfortable. Our vibration levels are different and people of different energy repel one another.

Do you find yourself in a nest of complainers? Are you surrounded by people who gripe? Then I've got some sobering news for you. We tend to be around people who are like us and to migrate away from those who are unlike us. One of the most poignant things about the Complaint Free phenomenon is the number of requests we receive from people saying something like, "Please send me purple bracelets right away; everybody I know complains all the time." When one of these requests comes in, and they do quite often, we smile and send the bracelets along without comment. We smile because we know that the person making the request probably also complains a lot and has no idea he or she is doing so. When they put on their own purple bracelet, these people take great leaps in compassion for others as they realize how much they, too, complain.

In *Illusions,* Richard Bach wrote a simple and profound truth: "Like attracts like." People who are alike, be they complainers or grateful people, attract one another. And people who are not alike repel one another. We are all energy beings, and energy that does not vibrate at the same frequency does not harmonize.

Thoughts, too, are energy. And you attract things that harmonize with your thought patterns and repel things that do not. Your words indicate, reinforce, and perpetuate your thoughts. So when you complain, you are actually repelling what you profess to want. Your complaining pushes away from you things that you say you'd like to have. I know of a group of women who get together each week to "support one another." This "support" consists primarily of complaining about men. From what I understand, their favorite themes are "men are selfish," "men don't want to commit," and "you can't trust men." Not surprisingly, none of these women is able to sustain a happy, healthy relationship with a man. Do they want such a relationship? Sure, but through their complaints they are sending out energy vibrations that "men are no good," causing no "good men" to appear in their lives. They are creating this reality with their complaints.

Several years ago, Gail and I met another couple who

had a son the same age as our daughter. We adults had a lot in common and the kids loved playing together, so our families spent a lot of time together. Over the course of several months, however, I noticed that neither Gail nor I looked forward to these get-togethers. One night Gail said, "I really like those two, but whenever she and I talk all she does is complain about him." I told her that complaining about the wife was what the husband also did most when he and I were away from the women.

We realized that during these gripe sessions the respective spouses not only complained about the other, they also seemed determined to help Gail and I find flaws in our own relationship. They tried to get us to focus on and talk about things we didn't like about each other. Misery not only loves company, it derives validation from it. Over time, we excused ourselves from spending time with this family and ultimately lost contact with them.

Gail and I have our challenges, as do any two people in any form of relationship. The person with whom you are in a relationship often brings up things that you need to own and, ultimately, heal. Gail and I resolve our issues by talking to each other rather than to other people. Talking to someone other than the person who brings up your unhealed feelings is triangulation. If you're unfamiliar with triangulation, it occurs when you have an uncomfortable situation with someone but discuss the problem with someone else rather than going to the person directly.

Healthy communication is talking directly and only to the person you have an issue with. Talking to someone else is complaining; it's triangulation and it perpetuates rather than solves the problem.

You may have experienced this in your own life. One of your children may be upset with one of their siblings but comes to you instead of the person with whom they are upset. You, the wise and benevolent parent, get involved by either advising the discontent child what to do or, worse, going to the other child yourself. In the short term, you may resolve the current situation, but you are not giving the children the tools they need to resolve future issues in their life. You are allowing the complaining child to remain a victim in the situation and are perpetuating this pattern for future challenges in the child's life.

You want to help and support your children, but when you try to resolve their personal issues with one another you are not modeling healthy communication. Further, you are unconsciously inviting your children to involve you regularly in future conflicts regardless of the scale or importance. Better to invite them to talk to one another, trust their own internal guidance, and resolve their conflicts. In so doing, you are giving them the gift of healthy communication. And you are helping them find their own power, which is an important gift.

Triangulation is rampant in some churches. I recently heard of one minister talking to another about the way a third minister was leading his church. After several minutes of this harangue, the listener—who had remained silent until that point—pressed the speaker button on his phone and called the minister being vilified. He then said, "Jim, this is Jerry. I'm sitting here with Mike and he was sharing some feelings he has about you and your church. I don't want to be a partner to triangulation and I know you'd love the feedback he's willing to share. So Mike, here's Jerry." Mike sat in silent shock, his face blazing. In that moment, Mike got the message very clearly that talking about someone behind their back was out of integrity. And Jerry drew a healthy boundary, ensuring that he would no longer be included in Mike's gossip.

This explains why I lump gossip in with complaining. Am I opposed to gossip? Absolutely not. As long as:

1. What you're saying about the absent person is complimentary.
2. You would repeat, word for word, what you are saying if the absent person were present.

If you can follow those two simple rules, gossip all you want. Try it. And no cheating by saying, "Isn't it great how poorly she dresses," calling it positive when you know that the underlying message is critical. It's the same thing. To quote a Southern colloquialism, putting icing on a pile of manure doesn't make it a cake. If you wouldn't say it directly to the person and that person feels complimented, it's gossip and complaining. Your mother was right—if you can't say something nice, don't say anything at all. You don't need that energy going out into your world.

If you're a person who normally gossips, you'll find that speaking only praise about those not present takes the fun out of it. In today's society, gossip usually means nit-picking. Do you know where the term "nit-picking" comes from? Lice eggs are called nits. To "nitpick" means to pick lice eggs from another's scalp. The thing about lice is that they love to move from one host to another. Don't pick nits, or you might become infested.

One of the main reasons we gossip or complain is to make ourselves look better by comparison: "At least I'm not as bad as [insert name here]." When I point out your faults, then I'm implying that I have no such faults so I'm better than you are.

Complaining is bragging. And nobody likes a braggart.

Here's another bit of sobering news: You wouldn't notice the faults in the other person if they were not also in you. Just as people who request purple bracelets for "all the whiny people around them" tend to be profuse complainers themselves, so too, you will find, the things that upset you about others are traits you share with them. You're just in the Unconscious Incompetence stage regarding that part of your personality. Noticing it in another is the Universe's way of inviting you to recognize it in yourself and heal it. If you want to point out something negative in another, do some digging, see if it's also within you, and be grateful for this chance to now be aware of the shortcoming and heal it within yourself.

And please don't let the corollary to this escape you. The good things, the things you admire in others, are appealing for the same reason. You see them in another because they are also within you. They are also attributes of who you are. The positive traits may lie dormant now, but if you focus on them, look for them within yourself, nurture and cultivate them, you will, through your attention, draw them to the surface.

You are not only creating your reality through your thoughts and words, you are also affecting those around you. The next time you are seated in an audience and the audience begins to applaud, notice something: If the clapping goes on long enough, the individuals will begin to clap to the same rhythm. They will syncopate. This is called entrainment. Human beings move toward harmony in their vibrations, and if the harmony cannot be reached, it will dissipate. When people entrain while clapping, the clapping tends to go on longer. If not, it ceases.

I've demonstrated this several times when speaking to large crowds. I've not told the audience why but instructed them to clap and keep clapping until I asked them to stop. Sometimes it happens within seconds, other times after a minute or two, but it always happens. The applause falls into a beat, a cadence; this group of individuals begins to clap as if they were synchronized human metronomes—they entrain.

My mother was one of four daughters in her family. She has told me that she and my aunts' menstrual cycles began happening at the same time each month. Just by being in close proximity to one another, their physiology would entrain. When my eldest aunt went away to college, in a short time her cycle shifted to match that of her roommate. When my aunt returned home for the summer, her cycle realigned with her sisters'. It is the nature of human beings to entrain, to synch up, to fall into the patterns of those around us.

Entrainment is a principle just as gravity is a principle. It's neither bad nor good—it simply is. And, just like gravity, it's always working. You are constantly synching up to those around you. You are entraining with them and they are entraining with you. When you are around others who complain, you will find yourself complaining more.

Becoming aware of the amount of complaining that goes on around you helps you realize that you might be experiencing it by attracting it through your own participation. This is all part of the process of transforming your life. And sometimes, as you change, you will shed some old relationships in the process. When I was going through the 21-day challenge, I found that I did well most of the time but ended up griping whenever I talked to one old friend of mine. After one fifteen-minute phone conversation in which I moved my bracelet four times, I said to myself, "If Scott wasn't so negative, I wouldn't be enticed to complain when we talk." The next time we spoke, I made a conscious effort to keep the conversation positive and found it was difficult. We actually had very little to say to each other. I found that our relationship was based on complaining and, being competitive people, we "one-upped" each other's gripes. If there was a Complaining Olympics, it would be touch and go as to which of us would take the gold.

In order to complete the challenge, I stopped taking his calls. "It's all Scott's fault," I'd say to myself, feeling very superior. Other people who knew Scott, however, did not experience him this way. With them, he was upbeat, optimistic, and cheerful.

Ouch.

I had to admit it was me. It was my negativity feeding the kvetching in our relationship, so during my hiatus from him, I worked to extricate complaining from myself rather than to blame it on him.

So reality check time. Would you say that the people with whom you spend most of your time complain frequently? If so, how's it going with your purple bracelet (or other self-monitoring device)? Are you finding that you, too, talk about things that you are unhappy with more than is healthy? Do you express grief, pain, or discontent on a regular basis? It's okay. If so, you're normal. But you can be more than normal; it's within you to be outstanding, and together we're going to get there.

I'm often asked, "How can I get my boss [or friend, lover, spouse, children, employees, etc.] to stop complaining?" The answer is: You can't. But didn't I say in a previous chapter that you can? Yes, and welcome to the great paradox of change. You can't make another person change. People change because they want to change, and trying to change someone only makes them cling to their existing behavior more tightly. To share another quote from my Southern heritage, "Never try and teach a pig to sing. It wastes your time and annoys the pig."

And a pig annoyed by you won't sign up for singing lessons given by you. The way to inspire change in others was summed up by Benjamin Franklin: "The best sermon is a good example." And Gandhi put it this way: "We must live what we want others to learn." If you want others to change, you must change first. Understand that I believe you have only the most noble of reasons for wanting them to change. But the fact that you are in this relationship with them means, to some extent, you are a contributing factor in the complaining that's happening. When bosses, parents, ministers, coaches, or family leaders request purple bracelets wanting to change those they lead, I often feel compelled to include a little note saying, "Warning, this will not work unless you do." I'm convinced this truly would have been just another doodad Sunday, as Marcia called it, if I had not stayed with it to prove that going 21 consecutive days without complaining was possible. If you want to lead someone to change, remember that a leader is out front, facing the frontier and blazing the trail for others to follow.

There is an old Russian proverb: "If you want to clean up the entire world, begin with sweeping your own doorstep." The change we seek is never "out there"— it is within ourselves. What we do does affect the world, because it affects those around us and this impact spreads.

Have you ever noticed the way conversations go when people get together? Someone may mention a book they recently read and the conversation shifts to books for a while. Or, if the book mentioned is about camping, the conversation may flow toward camping trips those gathered have enjoyed or found exciting. The conversation weaves from topic to topic like the 1980s video game Frogger, where the frog crosses a stream by first leaping to a floating log, then to a turtle's back, and then onto another log. Conversations move along similar lines. They are like a great symphony where a certain melody is played and repeated until there is a subtle shift by one of the instruments and a whole new melody unfolds.

The recovery literature of alcoholics and drug addicts says, "Our disease is progressive." So, too, is complaining. The next time you're in a group talking, notice when someone begins to complain. Complaining then becomes a competitive sport as one-upmanship sets in. The tone of the discussion becomes, "You think THAT'S bad, well, let me tell you about . . ." It starts off simply, no one attempting to sway the group toward griping, but soon the discussion becomes a contest as each person tries to outdo the others about bad things that have happened or are happening to them.

A great example of this aspect of our communication was lampooned by the British comedy troop Monty Python's Flying Circus in their skit "The Four Yorkshiremen," which was released on their 1974 album *Live at Drury Lane.*

In the sketch, the four sophisticated Yorkshire gentlemen are seated together enjoying some expensive wine. Their conversation begins positive, shifts subtly negative, and then, over time, the complaining one-upmanship becomes relentless.

It begins as one comments how, in years prior, he would have been lucky to have the price of a cup of tea. A second, wanting to top the first says that he would have been fortunate to have COLD tea.

The complaining revs up and their comments spiral into being ludicrous as each tries to prove that his life was the one of greatest hardship. At one point, one of the gentlemen tells of the poor condition of the house in which he was raised. The second Yorkshireman rolls his eyes and replies:

> "House! You were lucky to live in a house! We used to live in one room, all twenty-six of us, no furniture, half the floor was missing, and we were all huddled together in one corner for fear of falling."

Back and forth the lamentations continued. . . .

"Eh, you were lucky to have a room! We used to have to live in the corridor!"

"Oh, we used to dream of living in a corridor! We used to live in an old water tank on a rubbish tip. We got woke up every morning by having a load of rotting fish dumped all over us!"

"Well, when I say 'house' it was only a hole in the ground covered by a sheet of tarpaulin, but it was a house to us."

"We were evicted from our 'ole in the ground; we had to go and live in a lake."

"You were lucky to have a lake! There were a hundred and fifty of us living in a shoebox in the middle of road."

Finally, one of the characters trumps the competition by declaring, "I had to get up in the morning at ten o'clock at night, half an hour before I went to bed, drink a cup of sulfuric acid, work twenty-nine hours a day down in a mill, and pay the mill owner for permission to come to work. And when we got home, our dad and our mother would kill us and dance about on our graves singing Hallelujah."

Is the complaining competition something you want to win? Then fine, go ahead and gripe 'til everyone else gives in declaring you the greatest complainer in the world. This victory comes with prizes such as unhappy relationships rife with melodrama, health challenges, money worries, and an abundance of other issues. If these don't appeal to you, don't get involved when you hear griping. People are entraining you with their words and you are entraining them. When you are with others and the conversation begins to devolve into negativity, just sit back and observe it. Don't try and change others. If anyone asks why you're not complaining, just show them your purple bracelet and tell them you are "in training" to be a Complaint Free person.

CHAPTER 4

Waking Up

We have met the enemy and he is us.

—POGO

A young monk joined an order that required total silence. At his discretion, the abbot could allow any monk to speak. It was nearly five years before the abbot approached the novice monk and said, "You may speak two words." Choosing his words carefully, the monk said, "Hard bed." With genuine concern, the abbot said, "I'm sorry your bed isn't comfortable. We'll see if we can get you another one."

Around his tenth year in the monastery, the abbot came to the young monk and said, "You may say two more words." "Cold food," the monk said. "We'll see what we can do," the abbot said.

VOICES

I was recently traveling and bad weather had surrounded some of the destination airports, causing many flights to get canceled or delayed. I was sitting by the gate, having changed my flight to another one already, and was watching the unfortunate airline rep at the gate counter. She was being bombarded by a number of people who seemed to assume that the poor weather, flight cancellations, and everything else causing them grief was her fault, and each one in turn laid all of their grief on her and I could see she was being pushed to the brink.

A little ah-ha light bulb flashed in my mind and, since I am apt to follow my instinct, I stood up and took my place in the line of people intent on sharing their bad day with her. I patiently waited my turn, and when I was finally standing in front of her, her weary eyes looked up to me, her forehead creased with stress, and she asked, "May I help you, sir?"

I said, "Yes you can." I then asked her to act busy while I spoke to her. I told her I stood in line to give her a 5-minute

On the monk's fifteenth anniversary, the abbot said again, "You may now speak two words." "I quit," the monk said. "It's probably for the best," replied the abbot. "You've done nothing but gripe since you got here."

Like the young monk, you might not think you complain very often, but by now you are awakening to the fact that you do.

We've all experienced sitting, leaning, or lying on one of our arms or legs for a period of time and having it break. While she typed (I have no idea what she typed), I explained to her that while all of these people were intent on ruining her day, she had other people in her life who really cared about her and that she had passions in her life that gave her life meaning, which were far more important than what was happening here today. Given all of that, the stuff happening here wasn't important and shouldn't stress her out. We chatted back and forth for a few minutes as she continued to look busy.

After seeing her regain her composure, I knew she had to get back to her work and I wished her a great day, telling her it was time for the next customer. She looked up at me and I could see that her eyes were slightly welling up. "Thank you so much," she said. "I don't know how to thank you for this."

I smiled and told her the best way to thank me was to pass on the kindness to someone else when she had the opportunity.

—HARRY TUCKER, NEW YORK, NY

"fall asleep." When we shift our weight and the blood rushes back into the limb, it tingles. Sometimes the tingle is uncomfortable, even painful. The same is true when you begin to wake up to your complaining nature. If you're like most people, the realization of the frequency of your complaints can be shocking. That's okay. Just keep moving that bracelet and stay with it. Don't give up.

Remember, we're concerned only with complaints we speak. For the purposes of the 21-day challenge, we're working only to eradicate complaints that are expressed. If you think it, it's free. It doesn't count. You will find that as you say fewer and fewer complaints, your mind will produce fewer and fewer of them. We'll talk more about this later. For now, just focus on any griping that actually escapes your mouth.

Beware: The Conscious Incompetence stage is where I've seen a lot of people give up and go back to their old ways. The wave stops with them. The ripple no longer spreads. I mentioned in a previous chapter that I was very overweight as a child. In my senior year of high school, I finally lost in excess of 100 pounds. When friends asked what diet had achieved such great results for me, I would tell them, "The one I stuck with." I'd been on dozens of diets but finally stayed with one, and the results were great. So stick with it when you're shocked and embarrassed at how often you complain. I slipped and started over again. That's all it takes, starting over again and again—moving that bracelet. In the words of Winston Churchill, "Success is going from failure to failure without losing enthusiasm."

I'm a juggler. No, I'm not trying to be clever about how my life is so busy that I've got a lot of balls to keep in the air. I literally am a juggler; it's a hobby of mine. I learned to juggle from a book that came with three square fabric bags filled with crushed pecan shells. The shape of the bags and the contents were designed for one purpose: to keep them from rolling away when they were dropped.

The important and implicit message from the bags was: We ARE going to be dropped.

I juggle at my daughter's school functions and at church events. But I always decline invitations to juggle in talent shows. Juggling is not a talent; it's a skill. A talent can be cultivated and nurtured to full expression. A skill is something most people can learn if they will invest the time. I've taught people to juggle, and I always begin by handing them one of the nonrolling bags and telling them to drop it. Although confused, they do as I've asked. "Now pick it up," I tell them. They do. "Now drop it again." "Pick it up." "Drop it." "Pick it up." We'll go through this many times, until they begin to grow tired of the whole exercise. At this point, I'll ask, "Do you really want to learn to juggle?" If they say, "Yes," I tell them to get used to dropping and picking up the balls because they will do this thousands of times before they become proficient. Pick them up even when you're tired of dropping them and frustrated with yourself. Just keep picking them up.

Every time I've learned a new juggling maneuver, it's back to dropping and picking up again. The first time I tried to learn to juggle clubs, I spun one club in the air and its wooden handle smashed hard into my collarbone, raising a welt. I threw the clubs in a closet, deciding I could never learn to juggle clubs. A year or so later, I hauled them out and tried again. I can now juggle not only clubs, but knives and even flaming torches. Anyone who is willing to pick up the balls, clubs, knives, or torches over and over again can learn to juggle them. To become a Complaint Free person, you just move the bracelet and start over, and over, and over . . .

You might wonder, "When is what I'm saying a complaint and when is it just a statement of fact?" According to Dr. Robin Kowalski, "Whether or not the particular statement reflects a complaint . . . depends on whether the speaker is experiencing an internal dissatisfaction."* The words in a complaint and a noncomplaint can be identical; what distinguishes the two is your meaning, your energy behind them. The Conscious Incompetence stage is all about becoming aware of what you say and, more important, the energy behind what you're saying.

After more than two months of the 21-day challenge and countless starting over attempts, I finally made it to 20 days complaint free—one more day and I'd make it! I could see the finish line and I was closing in. During dinner with my family that night, I shared something that happened earlier in the day and, catching myself, gasped, "Oh no, was that a complaint?" Gail smiled and said, "Sweetheart, if you have to ask, it probably was a complaint." I moved my bracelet. Day 1, here I come—again. If you have to ask, it's probably a complaint. Start over

*Kowalski, R. M. (1996). "Complaints and complaining: Functions, antecedents, and consequences." *Psychological Bulletin*, page 181.

and remember that this is about transforming your life, not rushing through the experience. It's not a race, it's a process.

It's a complaint if you want the person or situation changed. If you want it other than how it is, it's a complaint and not just a statement of fact. As I write this, I'm sitting in the train station in San Jose, California. My train was scheduled to leave at 9:00 A.M. The time is now 10:30 and I've just been informed that the new departure time is 12:00 P.M.—three hours late. Depending on how you read what I've just written, you might think I'm complaining. But I know what my energy is about the situation. I am sitting on the train platform, enjoying the spring morning and a cup of cinnamon spice tea while sharing something I'm passionate about with you. I'm very happy. I am grateful. The train leaving late is a wonderful blessing. I get to do what I love in a beautiful environment.

Hmm, but what if I don't want to wait? Perhaps if I complain really loudly and angrily to the ticket agent, or if I complain to as many people as possible, I could hasten the train's departure. That would work, right? Of course not. And yet we see this behavior often. The train will get here when it's supposed to, and it will be the perfect time.

I was recently interviewed for a radio morning show. One of the announcers said, "But I complain for a living—and I get paid very well for complaining." "Okay," I said, "and on a scale of one to ten, how happy are you?" After a beat, he said, "Is there a negative number?" Complaining may benefit us in many ways, even financially, but being happy is not one of complaining's benefits.

We've discussed that we complain because we derive psychological and social benefits from doing so. Sociologists and psychologists theorize that we also complain as a way of making ourselves appear more discriminating. For example, even if the cuisine at a restaurant is excellent, a person might complain that the level of the food is not up to his or her standards. This is a way of letting everyone who hears know that they do in fact have high standards. The complainer is saying that they are an arbiter of fine food and is implying that their refined taste is derived from many high-class dining experiences. Like Rodney Dangerfield's character in *Caddy Shack* when he says to the waiter at the exclusive Bushwood Country Club, "Hey, tell the cook this is low-grade dog food," the complainer is saying, "I have so much sophistication, this fare doesn't impress me." Again, complaining is bragging.

Ask yourself: Do people who are confident and secure in themselves brag? The answer is no. People who have healthy self-esteem; people who enjoy their strengths and accept their weaknesses; people who are comfortable with themselves and don't need to build themselves up in the eyes of others—these people don't brag. They feel good about themselves and don't need to tell others how great they are. Similarly, they don't need to complain so as to derive the neurotic benefits of doing so. In *The Lazy Man's*

Guide to Enlightenment, Thaddeus Golas summed it up: "Loving yourself is not a matter of building up your ego. Egotism is proving you are worthwhile after you have sunk into hating yourself. Loving yourself will dissolve your ego: you will feel no need to prove you are superior."

A person who is insecure, who doubts their value and questions their importance, will brag and complain. They will tell of their accomplishments, hoping to see approval reflecting back to them in the eyes of their listeners. They will also complain about their challenges to get sympathy and as a way of excusing their not accomplishing something they desire. The truth is that they complain because they don't feel they deserve what they want. Their lack of self-worth leads them to push away with their complaints what they say they want.

Get this: Anything you desire, you deserve. Stop making excuses and move toward your dream. If you are saying things like "Men are commitment-phobic," "Everyone in my family is fat," "I'm not coordinated," "My guidance counselor told me I'd never amount to anything," and "My father abused me," you are making yourself a victim. Victims don't become victors. And you get to choose which you will be.

Complaining is like a note from Epstein's mother. Remember the show *Welcome Back Kotter?* Juan Epstein, one of the students in this classroom comedy, would often bring notes to school to get out of doing things. For example, a note might read, "Epstein can't take the test today because he was up all night discovering a cure for cancer," signed, "Epstein's Mother." Of course, Epstein wrote the notes himself to get out of taking tests and doing things. We complain to get ourselves out of taking risks and doing things. The complaints seem legitimate, but they're thin excuses, and like the notes on the show, they're actually written by the character presenting them: us.

Please know that I understand you may have had some tough, perhaps horrible, things happen to you. Many of us have. You can tell your story about them forever, be "right" about what happened, and let this be an excuse that limits you your entire life. Or you can think of a slingshot. What determines how far a stone from a slingshot will fly? The answer is: how far back you've pulled the band on the slingshot. If you study the lives of successful people, you will find that often their success was not in spite of their life challenges but because of them. They took what happened to them and used it to help them grow. They stopped telling everyone how much they were wronged and began to look for the blessings in their challenges. And looking, they found them. Their slingshot was pulled back far, but as a result, they soared even farther.

For a stone to fly from a slingshot, it must be released. You have to let it go. The same is true for the challenges and painful experiences in your life: Let them go!

When my first wife, Liese, left me she said that one of the main reasons was how insecure I was. I was very insecure and it drained her. I looked to her for approval and affirmation constantly. I understand this now. I attempted to make up for my insecurity by being loud, complaining, and critical of others. I was either telling everyone how great I was or criticizing others to make myself look good by comparison. I was in pain and directing it out at others. Remember: Those who hurt are hurting.

I finally looked at the word *insecure*. It's the opposite of *secure*. Being secure means being comfortable with something; accepting something as it is. For years, I had attempted to become a secure person by attempting to change nearly everything about myself. I began to understand that being secure with something means accepting it as it is, not trying to change it. My great learning in this experience was that to become a person who was no longer insecure, I WOULD HAVE TO BECOME SECURE WITH MY INSECURITY.

Rather than getting down on myself, making excuses for myself, or shifting the focus to others through criticism or complaining, I would have to accept those times of painful insecurity and support myself while going through them. When I felt uncomfortable, sad, weak, or unworthy (and I often did), I began to tell myself, "It's okay, just go ahead and feel how you feel. You're fine feeling this way."

It was a miracle. As I learned to be secure (comfortable) with my insecurity (feeling uncomfortable), the times of my discomfort became less frequent and short-lived. Just as you can't criticize another person to positive transformation, neither can you criticize yourself to positive change. Sometimes when my inner voice would be most critical, I would get my journal and let it spew. Rather than arguing back, I would then compliment what my angry voice had written. "Boy, you do a wonderful job of attacking me. I'm sure you do it because you want only the best for me. Feel free to express these thoughts anytime you wish." With no defense against them, my critical thoughts faded into nothingness.

We all have a gremlin in our head. The gremlin is that assaulting inner voice. I sought to befriend mine, and when I asked, he told me his name is Sylvester. When I think of Sylvester, I imagine the Tasmanian Devil from the Bugs Bunny cartoons. He's a snarling, whirling troublemaker whizzing about my brain creating chaos. When I attempted to quell his caustic remarks, he only got louder and more strident. Now, however, I encourage and compliment him. "You are really the best at finding fault in me, and I know you do it because you love me," I say. When I do this, I have a mental image of Sylvester standing there with a look of shock, not knowing what to do. Bewildered, with his lips puckered and his eyes darting back and forth, he is at a total loss as to what to say.

On a personal note, I'm eternally grateful to Liese. Her leaving me was the catalyst I needed to begin this quest. It was the catharsis that sent me deep into my soul and has allowed me to share what I've learned with the world. Thank you, Liese.

Don't complain to make yourself special; wake up to the truth that you already are special. Among the definitions for "special" are: "unique, distinctive, having a particular function." You are special. No one exactly like you has ever or will ever live. No one has your eyes, fingerprints, ear shape, or voice. You are as unique as your DNA. Scientists even say that no other person on the planet has your odor. How's that for special? You are a perfect expression of the Infinite. You are the Divine in human form. You are unique, and you have something wonderful to bring to this world at this time that only you can bring. You are perfect even with what you might call your imperfections.

As Sylvester and I became friends, I began to love those parts of myself that I used to loathe. Instead of faults, I embraced these attributes of myself as quirks, idiosyncrasies—things that made me me. To think I could change until I appreciated myself was folly. Constantly focusing on what was wrong with me ensured that I'd always find things wrong with me. There's that underlying theme again.

Shortly after I accepted the lead minister position at Christ Church Unity, a woman brought me a list of things she didn't like about the church. Wanting to make a good impression and one of my new congregants happy, I did what I could to change the things with which she was dissatisfied. Rather than coming to me later and saying, "Thank you, I'm now happy with this church," she brought me another list of complaints. When you express what you don't like, be it in yourself, your job, your family, your health, your finances, your church, or whatever, you will find more not to like. Remember, like attracts like. As you appreciate yourself, other people, and situations in your life more, you will attract more to enjoy.

The first time I appeared on *The Oprah Winfrey Show*, Oprah asked me, "Why do people complain about the weather? All the complaining in the world can't change it."

First, I'm not sure you can't change the weather. Now, before you write me off as a kook, let me tell you that a few years ago, I started telling friends that God and I have an agreement whereby I always get great weather. Last summer, we were planning a large church picnic and one of our leaders wanted to know what we'd do if it rained. "It's not going to rain," I said. "God and I have an agreement and I always get great weather." "Okay," she said, humoring me, "but what if it does rain?" "You didn't hear me—it won't rain," I said. "If we talk about it, it will rain, so let's not talk about it." Now, it's perfectly okay if you think it's just coincidence, but it didn't rain that day and my streak continues. And I'm not complaining.

Setting aside whether we have the ability to control the weather, why do we complain about it? Because it's safe; complaining is safe. It's a low-vibration-energy level of conversation. It's not threatening to another, because you're not calling them to higher levels of expression.

Another reason complaining is safe is that it may relate back to some racial memory combining theology and low self-esteem. We may have a fear that God (or, back when this fear began, the gods) might smite us for things going too well. In Pearl Buck's wonderful book *The Good Earth*, the hero, Wang Lung, is a Chinese peasant. His greatest desire is to have a son. Sons were highly valued in ancient China, and daughters were considered slaves you must feed and clothe until you turn them over to a man for marriage. Male children brought you wealth; females cost you.

To his great joy, Wang Lung's wife bears a son. When the couple walk through the streets carrying their newborn, they cover him up so the gods will not see him. They say, "It's only a simple slave, not a boy." They are afraid that the gods will take their child because they didn't deserve the great fortune of having a son.

Because of our low self-esteem, insecurity, and/or having been brought up with expectations that "good things don't last," we believe that God, the Universe, or whatever you call It is waiting to smite us if things go too well. If this is your theology, I honor your belief. For me, "God is love" and "God is waiting to bust you" don't work together. Our fear of Divine retribution makes us worry that if we talk of things going well they may turn bad. Actually, the opposite is true, as our fearful words call to us things we don't want.

There is a computer term, GIGO, which means "Garbage In, Garbage Out." It's based on the concept that computers are neutral—computers are impersonal and respond only to what is fed into them. And if you put garbage (poorly written code or commands) in, you will get garbage out (poor results).

When it comes to our lives, the opposite is true: Garbage Out, Garbage In. When you gripe and complain about things in your life (send Garbage Out), you are going to reap more of these challenges (Garbage In). The good news is that you are learning to catch yourself just as you speak and hold back or reframe your comments so as not to complain. You are now beginning to make the shift. You are moving into Conscious Competence.

PART 3

Conscious Competence

CHAPTER 5

Silence and the Language of Complaint

Anyone who uses the phrase "easy as taking candy from a baby" has never tried taking candy from a baby.

—AUTHOR UNKNOWN

The Conscious Competence stage is one of hypersensitivity. You begin to be aware of everything you are saying. You are moving your bracelet far less frequently because you are very careful when you speak. You are now talking in more positive terms because you are beginning to catch the words before they come out of your mouth. Your purple bracelet has gone from being a tool for realizing when you complain to being a filter through which your words pass before you speak them.

We received our purple bracelets and immediately realized that our conversations centered around sarcasm and criticizing others as well as each other. We didn't want to have to move our bracelets and start over, so we just quit talking for a day or two until we figured out ways to talk to each other that did not involve complaining.

—KIM MARTIN, KANSAS CITY, MO

One family who had taken the Complaint Free Challenge told me that during the Conscious Competence stage they would sit at their dinner table and often have nothing to say to one another. There would be periods of prolonged silence. And this is typical of a person or family at this stage of becoming Complaint Free. You really begin to live your mother's suggestion: "If you can't say anything nice, don't say anything at all."

Once the demand for our purple bracelets had risen to where we could have them custom-made, we considered dropping the word "spirit" from them. Although we are a church, we see the Complaint Free program as a nonreligious human transformation movement. Further, because it was picked up by so many other varied groups, as well as churches of all faiths, we didn't want people getting caught up in religion but to see this as a way of improving lives whether or not those involved had any religious affiliation.

I discovered that the word *spirit* comes from the Latin

spiritus, which means breath. In the Conscious Competence stage, one of the best things a person can do is to simply draw a deep breath rather than speaking out of hand. Complaining is a habit, and taking a moment just to breathe gives you a chance to select your words more carefully. As a reminder to take a breath rather than complain, we left the word "SPIRIT."

Silence affords us the opportunity to speak from our higher self rather than our human self. Silence is a bridge to the Infinite, and yet it is something with which many are uncomfortable. I can remember being at our lake house when I was a teenager and canoeing over to a small island about a mile from our home to camp alone. The silence gave me a chance to reconnect with myself. Once, as I was leaving for such a sojourn, I remember my father yelling to me from the bank:

"Will!?"

"Yes, sir."

"Where are you going?"

"Camping over at Count's Island."

"By yourself?"

"Yes, sir."

After a moment's pause: "Do you want a battery-powered TV to take with you?"

"No, sir. . . . Thank you."

After another pause: "A radio?!"

"No, thanks."

I will always remember how my dad shrugged his

shoulders, turned, and walked back to the house. I love my dad, but he's not much for silence. He even sleeps with a giant-screen TV blaring from the foot of his bed.

If you are a person who likes to pray, the Conscious Competence stage is a good time to deepen your prayer life. You've reached a point where you really don't want to move your bracelet, and you may wish to say a little prayer before speaking. Ask for guidance that the words coming from your mouth will be constructive rather than destructive. And, if no words come, remain silent. Back when I was selling radio advertising, I worked with a man who talked infrequently if at all. After getting to know him, I asked why this was. He told me, "It makes people think I'm smarter than I am." If you simply say nothing, people may at least give you credit for being smart. When we run off at the mouth, we don't make ourselves sound intelligent, we simply say that we're not comfortable enough with ourselves to let quiet reign, if even for a moment.

One of the ways we know we've met a person who is special to us is the amount of time we can be with that person with no words being spoken. We're simply comfortable in their presence and enjoy their company. A lot of mindless jabbering doesn't improve our time with them, it makes it less precious. Talking a lot sends a message to those around you that you're not comfortable with yourself.

Silence allows you to reflect and to carefully select

your words. It enables you to speak of things you wish to put your creative energy toward rather than allowing your discomfort to cause you to spout off a laundry list of grievances.

This stage of becoming complaint free was described in an e-mail we received from a lieutenant colonel at the Pentagon:

A quick update on how we're doing. All twelve bracelets are distributed among my co-workers, and so far there is one gal (who has always been quiet and low key) who is having some great success. I think she actually got into double digits :) The rest of us, however, are finding it more difficult than we even imagined. It HAS done something very important for us, though . . . when we are complaining, we know about it, we pause, we move our bracelets, and we restate what we were saying more positively. I haven't even gone an entire day yet, but I can see what a powerful communication tool it is for the synergy of an office. We are able to laugh at ourselves when we're complaining and challenge each other to find a better way. I'll send another update when someone reaches their goal. (Everyone is excited about expanding the challenge to more folks here in the Pentagon, so we're moving forward.) Have a Great Air Force Day!

—Cathy Haverstock

I mentioned before that the words you use when complaining will often be the same as those you use when you are not. It is your intention, your energy behind them, that will dictate whether or not you are complaining. Begin to notice how often and in what context you say the following:

- "Of course!"
- "Wouldn't you know it?"
- "Just my luck!"
- "This always happens to me!"

When something goes wrong and you say, "Of course!" or "Wouldn't you know it?" you are sending out a message that bad things are expected for you. The Universe hears this and sends you more.

I can remember the first time I decided to watch what I said very carefully, knowing it was a reflection of my thoughts and that my thoughts create my reality. I was using my wife's twenty-year-old pickup truck to retrieve some things I had in storage. Gail's old F-150 had several hundred miles on its original engine and got about twenty miles to the gallon—of oil! We were constantly putting oil in this old truck and kept a case of oil in the truck bed for adding more as needed.

As I left for this trip of a hundred-plus miles, I made sure the oil reservoir was filled and invited our dog Gibson to jump into the cab to keep me company. Gibson is an Australian kelpie and Gail named him. Gail said that if an Australian was going to be sleeping at the foot of her bed, she wanted it to be Mel Gibson.

It took several hours to drive from our home in Aynor, South Carolina, to the storage unit in Manning and load up my belongings. As we drove back, I decided to take a shortcut and headed toward Greeleyville. I used to live in Manning and knew the route to Greeleyville well. In fact, on weekends I used to ride my bike to Greeleyville and back for exercise. It is a stretch of about thirteen miles with little traffic.

As the sun began to set, the CHECK ENGINE light came on. My mode of thinking to that point was to say, "Oh, no! I'm in trouble." Instead, I turned to Gibson and said, "This is going to work out perfectly." Inside, I thought I was a little crazy. As I said, I know this stretch of road well. In the thirteen miles there are only a dozen or so homes, and I was not carrying a cell phone.

The truck sputtered and spat but continued on for a mile or more before the engine died. "This is going to work out fine," I said, attempting to sound as though I believed my words. The truck began to slow and finally stopped directly in front of one of the few homes on this stretch of road. "Of course!" I said, celebrating the moment and yet still amazed at how fortunate we had been. "Maybe the people are home and they'll let me use their phone," I thought. "I can call Gail and she can come get me." Then I remembered the loaded truck bed and thought, "I would rather be able to drive home tonight and not have to leave my stuff on the side of the road. I don't know how this is going to work out, but I'm going to believe it is."

Now remember, this was not my typical style of handling such things. In the past, I would have gotten out of the truck and probably done something helpful like swear and kick the tires. Instead, I closed my eyes and saw Gibson and me pulling into our driveway. In my vision, it was evening—just as it was at that time—and I was wearing the same clothes I was currently wearing. I allowed myself to sit a moment and clearly take in this image before walking up the driveway and ringing the doorbell.

When I heard people stirring inside the house, I again said, "Of course!" affirming that the people in this, the only house I could see for miles, were home just at the moment our truck broke down right out front. A man answered and introduced himself. When I explained that my truck had broken down and asked if I might use his phone, he peered into the darkness where the truck sat and asked, "What kind of truck are you driving?" "A Ford," I said. He smiled and said, "I'm the service manager at the Ford truck dealership. Let me get my tools and take a look."

"Of course!" I said as he went to get his tools. This was working out.

I held a flashlight as my new friend tinkered under the hood for fifteen minutes. He finally turned and said, "The problem is that there is something wrong with your fuel system. You need a small part—doesn't cost but a dollar or two, but I don't have one here at my house. What you've got," he continued, "is more of a plumbing problem than a mechanical problem."

"That's okay," I said. "Maybe I can just use your phone, then?" "Well," he said, "you've got a plumbing problem and my dad's visiting from Kentucky. My dad's a plumber. I'll go get him."

Scrubbing the fur on Gibson's neck and smiling deliriously, I said, "Of course!" as the man went into the house to retrieve his dad. A few minutes later, the father diagnosed the problem: "You need a piece of tubing about three inches long and a quarter inch wide," he said. "Like this one?" the son said, pulling the exact-size tube from his own toolbox. "That's it!" said the father. "Where did you find one?" "I don't know where it came from," the son said. "I found it on my workbench a month or so ago and just dropped it in the toolbox in case I ever needed it."

"Of course!"

Within moments, Gibson and I were back on the road. "What an experience," I said to Gibson. It all worked out. At that moment, the OIL light came on. We had sat for so long that the oil had drained from the truck and it was dangerously low. Seeing no homes anywhere, I began to get concerned but then stopped myself, saying loudly, "It worked once, it can work again!" As I drove, I again brought forth the image of Gibson and me pulling safely into our driveway that very night.

Turning the corner into Greeleyville, I pulled into what was then the only gas station in town. The owner was locking the door for the night as I pulled in. "Can I help you?" he asked. "I need oil," I said. Switching the station lights back on, he said, "Get what you need." I shoved my hands into my pants pockets and pulled out all the money I was carrying. At the rate the truck was dropping oil, I knew I might need as many as four quarts to make it home, and I had about $4.50 with me. I grabbed two quarts, all I could afford with the money I had, and laid them on the counter.

"Did you see the other brand?" the owner asked. "No," I said. He walked to the shelves with me following. "There it is," he said. "It's a good brand—better, I think, than the one you picked out, but I'm not going to carry it anymore, so it's on sale today—half price." Trying not to appear too thrilled, I swept four quarts up into my arms and headed for the counter. At 11:17 that very night, Gibson and I pulled safely into our driveway.

"Of course!"

One of the questions I'm often asked is "But don't you need to complain to get what you want?" You can best get what you desire by expressing what you want rather than complaining about the way things are. A couple of days ago, my cell phone rang and the caller ID read, "Unknown Caller." I was busy and did not answer, and whoever called did not leave a message. Nearly every hour after that, I received calls from the same "Unknown Caller" with no message left. Finally, I answered "Unknown Caller"'s call and heard a recorded message from my cell phone company: "This is an important message for Mary Johnson [not her real name]. . . . If you are

Mary, press one. If you are not this person, press three."

I pressed three, thinking the company would realize they'd called the wrong number and the calls would stop. They didn't. Almost every hour, the phone rang each time from "Unknown Caller." When I answered, I got the same friendly, computerized message. I pressed three repeatedly, but the calls continued.

People make mistakes. I know I do. And companies are just large groups of people doing the best they can. So, after a couple of days of hourly calls, I dialed the cell phone company, explained the situation, and was assured the calls would stop. The calls continued.

Prior to my making the 21 consecutive days Complaint Free, I probably would have called the company again, asked for a supervisor, and ripped into that poor soul. Further, I would have told everyone I came in contact with what a terrible injustice this was and how greatly I had been inconvenienced.

Instead, I called again and said to the customer-service person, "I know mistakes happen, and I know this isn't your fault. I'm committed to not getting these calls from your company anymore and am willing to work with you until we find the challenge and fix it together." Within ten minutes, she had found the issue (they had input my phone number as the other person's number in their computer) and the calls ceased.

I was able to get the result I wanted without having to raise my blood pressure or get angry. I also did not involve my friends, coworkers, and family in this issue by griping to them about it. Instead, I went to someone who could help me, explained what I wanted, and held that focus.

You have a right to get what you deserve. To achieve this, don't talk about or focus on the problem. Focus BEYOND the problem. See it resolved. Talk only about what you desire and only to someone who can provide it. You will shorten your wait time for what you seek and be happier in the process.

"But every great thing in our country began with people complaining . . . think about Thomas Jefferson and Martin Luther King!" an e-mail I received stated.

I realized that in one respect I agreed with the woman who sent the e-mail. The first step toward progress is dissatisfaction. But if we stay in dissatisfaction, we never move forward to brighter vistas. And those who complain as a matter of course chart their destination as being the same, unhappy port from which they sailed. Our focus must be on what we want to occur rather than what we do not. Complaining is focusing on what we don't want to occur.

Were the great leaders of the United Stages also great complainers? I'd have to say no. These important men and women allowed dissatisfaction to drive them to great visions, and their passion for these visions inspired others to follow them. Their relentless focus on a bright future raced the collective heartbeat of this nation. Their method of transforming our consciousness as a country and, as a result, our future, was best summarized by Robert Kennedy: "There are those that look at things the way they are, and ask why? I dream of things that never were, and ask why not?"

On August 28, 1963, the Rev. Martin Luther King, Jr., did not stand on the steps of the Lincoln Memorial and say, "Isn't it terrible how we're being treated?" No. He spoke words that struck a chord with our nation and still bring tears to the eyes of those hearing them nearly a half-century later. He did not focus on the problem, he focused beyond the problem. He declared, "I have a dream!" Dr. King created in our minds a vivid picture of a world without racism. He had "been to the mountain-top," and his powerful and inspiring words took us there as well.

In the Declaration of Independence, Thomas Jefferson did clearly state the challenges the colonies were having under the governance of the British Empire. However, his document, signed July 4, 1776, was not a litany of gripes. Had it been, it probably would have never caught the imagination of the world, garnered support from other countries, and unified the colonies.

The first paragraph of the U.S. Declaration of Independence reads:

When in the Course of human events it becomes necessary for one people to dissolve the political bands which have connected them with another and to assume among the powers of the earth, the separate and equal station to which the Laws of Nature and of Nature's God entitle them . . .

For a moment, imagine you are a colonist of one of the thirteen colonies and you try to take this in: ". . . *the separate and equal station to which the Laws of Nature and of Nature's God entitle them.*" At the time Jefferson wrote this, England was the world's greatest superpower, and he states without hyperbole that these fledgling and diverse colonies were "equal" to this political behemoth. You could have heard the collective gasp this inspired among the colonists, followed by the resulting swell of pride and enthusiasm. How could they ever aspire to such a lofty ideal as to be equal to England? Because *"the Laws of Nature and of Nature's God entitle[d] them."* This was not complaining; this was a compelling vision for a bright future. This was focusing beyond the problem.

Rosa Parks did not sit at the back of the bus and gripe to everyone about the injustice of having to sit there. Ms. Parks sat where she belonged, with everyone else regardless of skin color. She not only saw beyond the problem, she lived in the solution.

I hold a dream for such visionaries today. I can remember hearing for most of my life news of "peace talks" focused on the Middle East. As I've listened to what is discussed at the "peace talks," it appears they are more "war talks" or "if you'll stop doing this, then I'll stop doing that talks." United States presidents have brought together the leaders of the Middle East in an attempt to have them reconcile their differences. But the focus of these talks has been on "differences," and so the progress has been, in my opinion, minimal.

What if at these "peace talks" the leaders got together to talk about what it will be like when there is no more disharmony between them? What if they came together to build a collective dream of peaceful cohabitation and a mutual understanding of one another?

When these true "peace talks" occur, the rules will be simple. Rather than talking about what is going on in the present or what has happened in the past, the focus will remain exclusively on what it will be like when there is no more acrimony between them. They might ask, "What will peace between us look, feel, sound, and smell like? What will it be like when war and disagreement between us is such a distant memory we would have to consult history books because such a time is lost to us?"

The focus of the talks will be on only the desired outcome—peace. That's it. At these talks, one word will not be uttered: "how." The question "How will we get there?" will be agreed upon as off-limits at the outset. As soon as the two parties attempt to divine the road to their harmonious existence, questions of geographical boundaries, remunerations, disarmament, limitation of weapons, cultural and theological differences, and opposing perspectives of all types will bring their focus back on the current issues. And that focus will keep them in these problems.

Abraham Lincoln once said, "The best way to destroy an enemy is to make him a friend." The first step to such a transition begins in our own minds. And our words tell the world what we are thinking.

As you move through this stage of your transformation, it's fine to use terms such as "Of course!", "Wouldn't you know it?", "Just my luck!", and "This always happens to me!", but only when something you perceive as good happens. Say these as exclamations of thanksgiving when things go well for you.

I have a friend who has always said, "I'm the luckiest guy in the world—everything works out for me." He has a beautiful wife and family, he owns a successful business, he was a multimillionaire by age thirty, and he enjoys excellent health. You might say he's just lucky, with which he'd agree. I say it's his belief that he is lucky that makes him so. So why not try what has worked for him? When something goes well for you, no matter how small, say, "Of course."

Our words are powerful. And when we change what we say, we begin to change our lives. About a year ago, I was driving on the interstate and was in the passing lane because I was driving a few miles per hour above the speed limit. Ahead of me was a minivan driving about ten miles below the speed limit. My mind began to rant: "If they're going to drive below the speed limit, don't they know to stay in the right lane and let others pass?" A few days later, I found myself in the passing lane behind another cautious driver doing considerably less than the speed limit. Again I noticed the driver was behind the wheel of a minivan, and this time I vented aloud that I thought this was inconsiderate.

As I was driving a few days later with Gail and Lia, I was again slowed by a driver in the left lane traveling well below the speed limit in, you guessed it, a minivan. This time I voiced my complaint to my family. In the ensuing weeks, this situation repeated itself, and each time it was a minivan. I began to notice that minivans with certain symbols or stickers were the most egregious offenders. This became a pet peeve of mine, and I voiced this to everyone I knew. I thought it was funny, just a clever observation, but I did notice it was happening with greater and greater frequency. Finally, I began to understand that I had decided that "minivan drivers are rude and impede the flow of traffic." As I believed, so was it done unto me, and this became true for me nearly every time I drove.

I sought a way to reframe this observation and thought

of NASCAR. When there is a wreck or hazard at a NASCAR race, a pace car comes on the track to slow all the other drivers down. The drivers must fall behind the pace car until the hazard clears ahead, making it safe once again. "What if minivans are the pace cars of the interstate?" I thought. Maybe they are there to slow me down so I don't get a ticket or, worse, get involved in an accident. Whenever I was in the left lane behind a slower-moving minivan, I began to give thanks for them and to refer to them as pace cars. This became so habitual that I found myself forgetting they had another name and began to refer to minivans exclusively as pace cars. "Oops, there's a pace car up ahead," I'd tell my family, "we better slow down."

The interesting thing is that as I changed what I called them and began to appreciate minivans or pace cars for slowing me down, I found it atypical to be stuck behind one in the passing lane. Today, it's exceedingly rare for me to be slowed by a minivan on my commute, and when I do I give thanks for them.

By changing my mind about minivans and celebrating them as pace cars, I had changed what they were for me and they became a gift rather than a challenge. If you will begin to call the people and events in your life by names that spur positive energy in yourself, you will find that they no longer bother you and in fact can be a real boon for you. Change the words you use and watch your life change. For example:

Instead of . . .	*Try . . .*
Problem	Opportunity
Have to	Get to
Setback	Challenge
Enemy	Friend
Tormentor	Teacher
Pain	Signal
I demand	I would appreciate
Complaint	Request
Struggle	Journey
You did this	I created this

Give it a try. It may feel awkward as you begin, but watch how it changes your attitude about the person or situation. And as you change your language, the situation will change.

You can create the life you desire. I grew up believing that when we die, if we are fortunate, we will go to heaven. One day while reading the Bible I was struck by Jesus' comment "the Kingdom of God is at hand." And I began to wonder: "Maybe I have already died and this IS heaven." As I pondered this, I thought of John Milton's quote "The mind is its own place and in itself, can make a Heaven of Hell, a Hell of Heaven." Perhaps this is heaven, or at least I could make it so.

When asked how they are, I have heard people groan sarcastically, "Another day in paradise." I decided to adopt this as my own genuine answer to this question. Not being sarcastic, but sincerely responding, "It's another day in paradise," when asked about my well-being. It was uncomfortable at first, but it has now become second nature. I've noticed that this comment makes others smile brightly, and it reminds me that I have a choice in that moment to be happy or sad; to be in heaven or hell.

You have a choice with the words you use to create the life you live.

Choose wisely.

CHAPTER 6

Critics and Supporters

Criticism comes easier than craftsmanship.

—ZEUXIS

Criticism is complaining with a sharp edge. It is typically directed at someone with the intent of belittling that person. Some think criticism is an effective way of changing another's behavior. However, it actually tends to have the opposite effect.

I mentioned in the introduction to this book that my family and I recently lived in a home on a curved road where, sadly, our dog Ginger was killed. Because we lived just a short distance from where the speed limit changed from 25 to 55 mph, people were often driving quite fast in front of our home. I was bothered by this, especially after Ginger's death.

VOICES

I was doing very well with becoming complaint free. I had strung a series of days together and could tell it was changing my life.

My husband insisted that I stop. He said I was simply not as much fun to be around. I guess he thinks complaining is fun and I wouldn't join in with him and his griping anymore.

This makes me sad.

—NAME WITHHELD

Often, I would be on my riding mower cutting the grass as the cars sped by. I would shout at the drivers to slow down. Sometimes I would not only shout but wave my arms in an attempt to get them not to speed. To my increased irritation, I found they rarely slowed and averted their eyes so as not to look at me as they raced by. There was a yellow sports car that was the worst offender, and no matter how I screamed and flailed my arms, the young woman drove at a dangerously high rate of speed in front of our house.

One day, as I was cutting the grass in the backyard and Gail was in the front planting some flowers, I noticed the yellow speedster approaching, fast as usual. I did nothing, because I felt anything I did to try to slow her down would be futile. When the car passed in front of the house, I noticed a flash from the driver's brake lights and the car slowed to a safe speed. I was amazed. This was the first time I'd ever seen the sports car not blaze by at breakneck speed. I also noticed that the young woman, who normally looked quite sullen, was smiling. Curious, I turned off the mower and walked to the front yard and asked Gail what had happened to slow the woman down. Without looking up, Gail said, "It was easy. I just smiled and waved at her." "What?" I said. "I smiled and waved at her like she was an old friend, and she smiled back and slowed down," Gail said.

For months, I had tried getting the woman to slow down by being critical of her. I was intent on letting her know that she was wrong for driving as she did. Gail had treated her with kindness and the driver had responded with kindness. As I thought about this, it made sense. The woman driving by could not have heard my tirade over the sound of the mower, and my gestures probably just made me look silly. To her, I was the angry guy on the mower. No wonder she wanted to avoid eye contact and drive hastily past. Gail, on the other hand, she saw as the nice, neighborly lady who treated her as a friend. I had been a critic, whereas Gail had treated her with appreciation. I never saw the yellow sports car speed by our house again. Instead, it always slowed to a safe speed until it was past our neighborhood.

No one likes to be criticized. And rather than diminish what we criticize, our criticism often only serves to expand it. To criticize means to find fault with someone or something. And when we criticize someone, they feel a need to justify their behavior. Justification arises when a person feels that an injustice has occurred. To them, the criticism is an injustice and they strike back with whatever means they have. In this case, when I yelled at her the young woman continued to speed as a means of justifying her right to do so. There was a much more effective and loving way of getting her to slow down, and Gail had modeled it for me.

Great leaders know that people respond much more favorably to appreciation than criticism. Appreciation inspires a person to excel so as to receive more appreciation. Criticism tears someone down, and when we debase someone we actually give that person implicit permission to act in similar ways in the future. If we criticize a person as being lazy, for example, they then accept this as reality when relating to us. This gives them unspoken permission to act as a person worthy of the label "lazy" and the behavior repeats itself.

The number-one need we all have is to be recognized, to be valued, to feel we matter. Even if we are introverted by nature, we still want attention from others, especially those we consider important to us. Even when the attention is negative, such as criticism, the person will often repeat the behavior just to get the attention they desire. Rarely is this a conscious maneuver; rather, it is done without thinking. We all want attention and will get it however we can. And if the attention is critical, the person will adjust down to meet the expectations of the critic.

Attention drives behavior. Let me say that again: "Attention drives behavior." As much as we'd like to feel it's the other way around, it's not true. If we criticize someone, we are inviting future demonstrations of what we are criticizing. This is true for your spouse, your children, your employees, and your friends. In George Bernard Shaw's play *Pygmalion*, Eliza Doolittle explains this phenomenon to Colonel Pickering: "You see, really and truly, apart from the things anyone can pick up (the dressing and the proper way of speaking, and so on), the difference between a lady and a flower girl is not how she behaves, but how she's treated. I shall always be a flower girl to Professor Higgins, because he always treats me as a flower girl, and always will; but I know I can be a lady to you, because you always treat me as a lady, and always will."

We are far more powerful in the creation of our lives than we realize. Our thoughts about people determine how they will show up for us and how we will relate to them. Our words let the other person know our expectations of them and their behavior. If the words are critical, then the behavior will mirror the expectation represented by what we say.

We all know of parents who focus on a child's poor marks rather than celebrating their good grades. The child brings home a report card with four As and a C and the parent says, "Why did you get a C?" The focus is on the one average grade rather than the four excellent ones. A while back, our daughter Lia's grades began to slip and we, being intelligent, loving, and helpful parents, focused on the poor grades in an attempt to inspire her to improve. To our surprise, her other grades began to slip as well. In time, Gail and I realized that her grades were exactly that, "her" grades. We began to praise her good marks and simply ask if she was satisfied with her report card. If Lia said "Yes," even if she had grades below what we felt she should earn, we let it go. Very soon, her grades picked up and she's now had several years of straight A's.

"It's my job to complain and be critical." I've heard this from a number of people in the media and it saddens me. I have a degree in broadcast journalism and was taught that a journalist's job is to report the facts, to explain what is happening. However, some in the media seem to feel that it is their job to whip people into a lather. This is done to get people to listen to or watch the news or to buy a paper. It's about ratings and revenue. It is important that we be informed but not manipulated, and criticism is often used as a way to sway another person.

I'm not saying that we should not have movie, book, and theater critics. A good critic (I prefer the term "reviewer") can save us time and money by letting us know whether a film, book, or play is worthy of our time and money. There is actually one movie reviewer who I find tends to like the same movies I do, and since his job is to see all the movies and report on them, I find his input valuable and trust him. When we read a review, we can all tell if the person is a reviewer or a critic. Last night at dinner, I read a review of a movie opening this week. The critic's review was lost in long, arcane words and esoteric film references that told little about the film and seemed to say, "See how smart I am?"

As with other complaining, criticizing can be a form of bragging—a way of saying, "My tastes are so refined that what you're offering does not measure up." Did you see the movie *Hitch*? In it, Kevin James's character is dating a young heiress who is surrounded by haughty snobs. At one party, there are discussions of restaurants, movies, plays, and art gallery openings, all of which are labeled "disgusting" by two young men. They are saying, "Everything is disgusting to us—nothing measures up because we are so sophisticated."

Listen carefully to your words during the Conscious Competence stage and check yourself for criticism. Know that you are perpetuating what you criticize. When I was in this phase of the program, I called it the "I don't want to move my bracelet" stage. I would begin to speak and, noticing a criticism forming in my mind, I would simply state, "And I'm not going to move my bracelet." Try that when you catch yourself about to speak out of integrity— simply say, "I'm not going to move my bracelet."

Another healthy thing to do during this stage is to solicit a "Complaint Free Buddy." Find someone who is also working on this challenge and encourage each other. Note: This is NOT a person to watch like a hawk to see when they complain, criticize, or gossip. You are NOT to point out when they complain. If you do, you're complaining and you should move your bracelet. Rather, this is a person you can share your successes with and who will encourage you to continue if and when you have to start over. Find a person who can help you reframe the situations in your life in a positive manner, someone who will be on "blessing patrol" for you, helping you seek out the good in whatever situation you are facing. You need a cheerleader—someone to encourage you when you're tempted to quit; a person who wants you to make it.

About eight years ago, I met a man who helped someone he loved dearly reframe what many would think was a tragic situation. And it all started one day when I saw a sign along the side of the road.

The sign was created from a tattered piece of cardboard and stapled to what looked like one of those sticks given out at the hardware store to stir paint. As I was about to cross the causeway over the Waccamaw River, just outside Conway, South Carolina, I noticed the sign. There, shoved into the ground amid the litter and the fire-ant beds, it invited me to

HONK IF
YOU'RE HAPPY

I shook my head at the naïveté of the sign's creator and continued driving—my horn silent.

I snorted to myself, "What a bunch of fluff." Happy?

What is "happy"? I'd never known happy. I'd known pleasure. But even in my moments of greatest pleasure and fulfillment, I found myself wondering when something bad was going to happen to bring me back to "reality." "Happy is a scam," I thought. Life is painful and challenging, and if things are going well, there is something around the next corner that is going to snap you out of the "happy fantasy" really fast. "Maybe you're happy after you die," I thought, but I wasn't even sure about that.

On a Sunday a couple of weeks later, Gail and Lia—who was two at the time—were riding in the car with me down Highway 544 to Surfside Beach to see some friends. We were singing along to a cassette of *Favorite Kids' Songs*, laughing and enjoying our time together. As we neared the causeway to cross the Waccamaw, I saw the sign again and, without thinking, tapped my horn.

"What?" Gail asked. "Was there something in the road?" "No," I said. "There's this sign on the side of the road that says, 'Honk if You're Happy.' . . . I felt happy, so I honked."

The sign made perfect sense to Lia. Children don't have concepts of time, taxing responsibilities, disappointment, betrayal, or any of the other constraints or wounds that adults carry. To her, life is in the moment and the moment is meant for happiness. When the next moment arrives, it too is meant for happiness. Honk and celebrate this happy moment.

Later that day, as we made our way home and passed

the sign, Lia shrieked, "Honk the horn, Daddy, honk the horn!" By this time, my pleasant perspective of earlier that day had shifted from looking forward to time with friends and enjoying my family. I had begun to think of the many things that awaited me at work the next day and to dread most of them. My mood was anything but happy, but I still tapped the horn to appease my daughter.

What happened next I'll never forget. Deep inside and just for a moment, I felt a little happier than I had just seconds before—as if honking the horn made me happier. Perhaps it was some sort of Pavlovian response. Maybe hearing the horn caused me to conjure up some of the good feelings I had when I last honked.

From that point on, we could not pass that particular stretch of highway without Lia reminding me to honk. I noticed that each time I did, my emotional thermostat rose. If on a one-to-ten scale I was feeling an emotional two, when I honked the horn my happiness grew several points. I noticed that this happened each time we passed the sign and honked the horn. I began to honk whenever I passed the sign, even if I was alone in the car.

One day, Gail arrived home choking back laughter. Sensing it had to do with Lia and not wanting to embarrass her, I waited until she had gone to play in her room and asked Gail what was so funny. Gail burst into peals of laughter. Trying to catch her breath, she told me what had happened. "This afternoon," she began, "I was driving and talking with Lia when I made a lane change and accidentally cut someone off. The car had been in my blind spot and I'd not seen it. I nearly ran the poor driver off the road."

Again she laughed. I was missing the humor in the story.

Gail continued, "The driver of the other car got so mad that he whipped up alongside us, shot up his middle finger, and leaned on his horn."

We all make mistakes when driving. This could have been a dangerous one, so I was feeling concern not only for my wife and daughter but also for the driver of the other car. I thought that this was no laughing matter and that my wife must have somehow lost her mind. "What's so funny about this?" I demanded to know.

"When the man honked the horn," Gail continued, sensing my concern and trying to compose herself, "Lia pointed to the man and said, 'Look, Mommy, he's happy!'"

It took a second for it to sink in and then I, too, exploded with laughter. What a precious perspective a child has. Thanks to our experiences with the sign, the honking of a horn meant only one thing to her: The person was happy.

The positive feeling I had when I honked at the sign began to extend. I found myself looking forward to that particular section of road, and even before I reached the sign, I noticed I began to feel happier inside. In time, when I turned onto Highway 544, I noticed that my emotional setpoint would begin to rise. That entire 13.4-mile stretch began to become a place of emotional rejuvenation for me.

The sign was on the shoulder of the highway next to some woods that separated nearby homes from the causeway. In time, I found myself wondering who put up the sign and why.

At that time in my life, I was selling insurance to people in their homes. I had an appointment to meet with a family who lived about a mile north of Highway 544. When I got to their home, I was told by the mother that her husband had forgotten our appointment and that we would need to reschedule. For a moment, I felt dejected, but as I was driving out of the housing development, I realized that I was on the backside of the woods that bordered the highway. As I drove along the road, I estimated where I was in relation to the "happy" sign, and when I felt I was close, I stopped at the nearest home.

The house was a one-story, gray, manufactured home with dark red trim. As I climbed the cinnamon-colored stairs of the deck leading to the front door, I noticed that the home was simple but well cared-for. I began to prepare what I would say if someone answered the door. "Hi," I would say. "I saw a cardboard sign on the highway on the other side of these woods and was wondering if you know anything about it." Or maybe: "Are you the

'Honk if You're Happy' people?" I felt awkward, but I wanted to know more about the sign that had had such an impact on my thinking and my life. When I rang the doorbell, I didn't get a chance to say any of the opening questions I had practiced.

"Come in!" the man said with a broad, warm smile. Now I really felt awkward. "He must be expecting someone else," I thought, "and he thinks I'm that person." Nonetheless, I entered the home and he shook my hand. I explained that I had driven the highway near his home for more than a year and had seen a sign that said, "Honk if You're Happy." By my estimation, his house was the one closest to the sign and I wondered if he knew anything about it. His smile broadened, and he told me he had put the sign up more than a year ago, and that I was not the first to stop in and inquire about it.

As I heard a couple of horn blasts from a car in the near distance, he said, "I'm a coach at the local high school. My wife and I enjoy living here near the beach and we love the people. We've been happy together for many years." His clear blue eyes seemed to penetrate mine. "A while back, my wife became ill. The doctors told her there was nothing they could do. They told her to get her affairs in order and gave her four months to live—six months at the outside."

I was uncomfortable with the brief silence that followed; he wasn't. "First we were in shock," he said. "Then we got angry. Then we held each other and cried for what seemed like days. Finally, we accepted that her life would be ending soon. She prepared herself for death. We moved a hospital bed into our room and she lay there in the dark. We were both miserable.

"One day I was sitting on the deck while she tried to sleep," he continued. "She was in so much pain, it was hard for her to sleep. I felt I was drowning in my despair. My heart ached. And yet as I sat there, I could hear the cars crossing the causeway to go to the beach." His eyes drifted up to the corner of the room for a moment. Then, as if remembering he was talking to someone, he shook his head and picked up the story: "Did you know the Grand Strand—what people call the sixty miles of beach along South Carolina's coast—is one of the top tourist destinations in the United States?"

"Um . . . yes, I did know that," I said. "More than thirteen million tourists a year come to the beaches around here."

"That's right," he said. "And have you ever been happier than when going on vacation? You plan, you save, and then you go off to enjoy some time with your family. It's great." A long honk from a passing car punctuated his point.

The coach thought for a moment and then continued, "It hit me as I sat there on the deck that, although my wife was dying, happiness didn't have to die with her. In fact, happiness was all around us. It was in the millions of cars that passed just a few hundred feet from our house every day. So I put up the sign. I didn't have any expectations for it; I just wanted the people in their cars not to take this moment for granted. This special, never-again-to-be-repeated moment with the ones they care for most should be savored and they should be AWARE of the happiness in the moment."

Several honks sounded from different horns in rapid succession. "My wife began to hear the honks," he said, "just a few here and there at first. She asked me if I knew anything about it, and I told her about the sign. In time, the numbers of cars honking began to grow and they became like medicine for her. As she lay there, she heard the horns and found great comfort in knowing that she was not isolated in a dark room dying. She was part of the happiness of the world. It was literally all around her."

I sat in silence for a moment, trying to take in what he had shared. What a touching and inspiring story. "Would you like to meet her?" he asked. "Yes," I said with some surprise. We'd spoken for so long about his wife that I began to think of her more as a character in a rich and wonderful story rather than a real person. As we walked down the hall to their room, I braced myself, not wanting to appear shocked by the sick and dying woman who awaited me. But as I entered, I found a smiling woman who seemed to be playing sick rather than someone genuinely near death's door.

Another honk from outside and she said, "There goes the Harris family. It's good to hear from them again. I've missed them." After we were introduced, she explained that her life was now as rich as ever before. Hundreds of times a day and throughout the night, she heard the chirps, trumpets, bleats, blasts, and roars of horns telling her that there is happiness in her world. "They have no idea I'm lying here listening," she said, "but I know them. I've gotten to where I know them by the sounds of their horns." She blushed and then continued, "I've made up stories about them. I imagine the time they're having at the beach or playing golf. If it's a rainy day, I imagine them at the aquarium or shopping. At night I imagine them visiting the amusement park or dancing under the stars." Her voice trailed off and then, falling asleep, she said, "What happy lives . . . what happy, happy lives."

The coach smiled at me and we both rose and made our way out of the bedroom. In silence he walked me to the door, but as I was leaving, a question came to me. "You said the doctors gave her six months to live—max, right?" "That's right," he said with a smile that knew my next question. "But you said she was sick in bed for several months before you put up the sign." "Yep," he said. "And I've driven by and seen the sign now for well over a year," I finished.

"Exactly," he said, and then added, "Please come back and see us again soon."

The sign was up for another year and then, one day, it was suddenly gone. "She must be dead," I thought sadly as I drove by. "At least she was happy in the end and beat the odds. Wouldn't her doctors be surprised?" A few days later, I was taking 544 to the beach and, for the first time, I felt sadness rather than happiness as I approached the bridge. I checked again, wondering if the wind or rain had simply finally ruined the little handmade cardboard sign. But it was indeed gone. I felt dark inside.

As I drew near the causeway, I noticed something that lifted my spirits. Where the little cardboard and paint-stick sign once stood, there was now a new sign. It was six feet wide and four feet high with a bright yellow background bordered with bright, flashing lights. On both sides of the new sign, in large illuminated letters, was the familiar "Honk if You're Happy!"

With tears in my eyes, I leaned on my horn to let the coach and his bride know I was passing. "There goes Will," I imagined her saying with a wistful smile.

With the support of her loving husband, rather than focusing on what her reality was—a reality confirmed by medical experts—this wonderful woman had focused on the good around her. And, in so doing, she had beaten the odds, embraced life, and touched millions of people.

You can be just such a support for another person, a person seeking to change their life by ceasing to complain. Find someone you can cheer on and support and who will do the same for you. Together, you can make it happen.

PART 4

Unconscious Competence

CHAPTER 7

Mastery

Do everything without complaining.
—PHILIPPIANS 2:14

There are several species of fish known as blind cave fish. Most of them can be found in the United States in the limestone cave regions of the Mississippi Delta. Blind cave fish grow up to five inches in length and have little or no pigmentation. In addition to their pale skin, all but one of the species have no eyes. Scientists conjecture that many years ago these fish may have been trapped by shifts in landmass or water channels and became cave-bound. Surrounded entirely by darkness and unable to see, the fish adapted to their surroundings. These species of fish now thrive in total darkness.

Over generations of reproducing offspring, the pigmentation to protect their skin from the sun was left

VOICES

Four years ago, my twenty-three-year-old son (my oldest), a police officer, suffered a bleed in his brain while driving. Without going into details, it has been a long road, but one that my whole family has faced with trust in God and unconditional love.

Ben's recovering (all the docs said he wouldn't make it) and he accepts his disabilities with a peace that is such a lesson for us all. God's grace is active and growing in him.

He has mild aphasia, right-side weakness, and some slower processing, yet he continues to improve—all without complaining. Thus the reason for the bracelets. If Ben can accept his cross without complaining, surely the rest of us can. I want people who have helped Ben in his recovery to all get a bracelet.

Thank you so much and continued GOOD LUCK with your mission. You and your church have made an impact!

—NOREEN KEPPLE, STONINGTON, CT

behind because it was no longer needed. Similarly, over time, the blind cave fish began to produce fry without eyes. With no light and no ability to see anything, their bodies adapted to the environment and stopped producing pigmentation or eyes.

After you have gone the months it takes to become a Complaint Free person, you will find that you will have changed. Just as, over generations, the blind cave fish left behind what it no longer needed, you will find that your mind no longer produces the deluge of unhappy thoughts you used to live with. Because you are not speaking them, you have no outlet for them, and the complaint factory in your mind closes down. You have shut off the spigot and the well has dried up. By changing your words, you have reshaped the way you think. It has now become Unconscious (you don't notice) for you to be Competent (not complain). And as a result, you are a different person. You are a happier person.

When we began the Complaint Free program, we decided to give a "Certificate of Happiness" when someone made 21 consecutive Complaint Free days. We chose to give a "Certificate of Happiness" rather than a "Complaint Free" certificate, because we knew that eliminating griping would have a sweeping and powerful effect on a person's consciousness. Rather than just changing behavior, not complaining changes one's mind and life. When you have successfully completed your 21 days, please go to our Web site, www.AComplaintFreeWorld.org, and we'll be happy to send you a certificate to celebrate your transformation.

In the Unconscious Competent stage, this post-21-day phase, you are no longer an "ouch" looking for a hurt. Rather, your thoughts are now on what you want, and you are beginning to notice that not only are you happier, but the people around you seem happier. You are attracting upbeat people, and your positive nature is inspiring those around you to even higher mental and emotional levels. To paraphrase Gandhi, you have become the change you wish to see in the world. When something goes well for you, your immediate response is "of course." And when a challenge presents itself, you don't give it any energy by speaking about it to others; rather, you begin to look for the blessing in it. And seeking, you find.

Another thing you will notice is how uncomfortable you now feel when anyone around you begins to complain. It's as if a very unpleasant odor has suddenly wafted into the room. Because you have spent so much time checking yourself against complaining, when you hear it coming from someone else it's like a cacophonous cymbal during a moment of sacred silence. Even though their griping isn't pleasant for you to hear, you won't feel compelled to point it out to the other person. Rather, you'll simply observe it and, because you neither criticize nor complain, the person won't need to justify their behavior and it will stop quickly.

You will begin to feel gratitude for the smallest things—even things you used to take for granted. For myself, I can remember thinking, "If I knew the last time I brushed my hair was going to be the LAST time I'd brush my hair, I would have enjoyed it a whole lot more." (If you don't understand this comment, look at my photo on the book jacket.) As you settle into being Unconscious Competent, your default mind-set will be one of appreciation. You will still have things you desire for yourself, and that's good. Now, with your newfound positive energy, you can hold an image in your mind of what you yet desire, knowing that it is, even now, moving toward you.

Your financial situation may improve as well. Money is, in and of itself, without value. Money is slips of paper and coins that represent value. As you begin to value yourself and your world more, you will vibrate at a level that attracts greater financial benefits for yourself. People will want to give and provide things for you that you may have had to pay for in the past. I know of a man who receives a number of professional services free simply because the people providing these services like him and wish to support him. The same can happen for you. The key is to watch for the smallest of these and be grateful. If someone holds open a door for you, or offers to carry something for you, count it as an abundant blessing of the Universe and, in so doing, you will attract more.

Positive, happy people are simply more enjoyable to be around. Now that you are such a person, another way your finances may improve is through pay raises and increased job security.

In our jobs, we are paid for our ability to do or make certain things. Our degree of competence in our vocation dictates in large part how well we are paid. But a person who shines sunlight and joy on the office is worth their weight in gold. I know a business in Seattle, Washington, that had a receptionist named Martha. Martha had the widest, brightest, and most sincere smile I've ever seen.

She was always complimentary, genuinely happy, and willing to do anything for anyone. You could feel her presence in the office, and everyone there found themselves more cheerful and productive because of Martha.

A while back I stopped by this business to visit some friends. Something was different. It was as if someone had painted the walls a darker color, or perhaps the lighting had gone bad. That's what it felt like as I stood in the reception area. Then I realized that Martha was gone. "Where's Martha?" I asked. "She was hired away," someone said, "for more than twice what we were able to pay her." After looking around for a moment, she added, "The other company got a deal."

Martha's happy, upbeat personality radiated out to everyone at this company, and her leaving brought the overall level of happiness and productivity down. Salespeople said that client complaints increased both in number and vehemence when Martha was not there to answer the phone.

Your attitude, which is an outward expression of your inner thoughts, dictates how people will relate to you. Not only people, but animals as well. As I write this, our two dogs are barking excitedly at the UPS truck that has driven into our neighborhood. Gibson and Magic are not barking to defend their territory. They're not barking to prevent the UPS driver from stopping at our house, but rather in hopes that he WILL stop at our house. Unlike other delivery drivers who are afraid of or don't want to deal with dogs, our UPS driver has decided to learn the names of every dog on his route. He even carries dog treats for them. It may sound silly, but our dogs love the UPS driver, we love our dogs, and so we love the UPS driver. Our driver's simple intention of being a happy and helpful person has endeared us more to UPS than a thousand "What can Brown do for you?" television commercials.

If he aspires to management, I can see this driver leading UPS someday. We all want to be around people who make the everyday extraordinary. And those people are most likely to ultimately get promoted.

One of the greatest gifts of becoming a Complaint Free person is the impact you will have on your family, both in the present and in the future. For better or worse, we tend to model those around us. As we discussed in a previous chapter, we entrain to the energy of others and especially to those we consider authority figures, such as our parents.

I can remember my dad in the kitchen. Whenever he cooked, he took a dish towel and draped it over his left shoulder; he called it his "left-shoulder cooking towel." The towel hung there should he need to remove something hot from the stove or to wipe something from his hands. Today, whenever I'm in the kitchen, you will always find me with my own "left-shoulder cooking towel." And it's never on the right shoulder, always the left. That's how Dad did it; that's how I do it. Perhaps my dad had seen his father do this and was following after him—who knows? All I know is that I picked this up from him. He never sought to instill this idiosyncracy in me, but his behavior did so. And I know that whether I intend to or not, I'm passing along things to Lia all the time.

I realized that before we adopted a Complaint Free lifestyle, I was teaching Lia that being at the family dinner table was a time to gripe and gossip. I was modeling for her that this is how people act. I'm so grateful now that our supper table is where we talk about blessings and bright vistas. This is what I want to pass on to her so she'll model this for her children and their children after them. Let family time be joyous and happy, not a time to vent about how things didn't go your way that day. I'm convinced that our lives are better because we're not searching out (and thereby finding) negative things every day to make sure we have dinner conversation that night.

By being a noncomplaining person, you draw more of what you want to you with less effort. Remember the woman from my church with the lists of complaints? After I went through a couple of her lists, I realized that no matter what I did she was going to find fault with more things. Without intending to, I began to have a strong mental resistance to anything she asked me to do and to resent her because nothing we did seemed to satisfy her. Ideas she proposed, even good ones, were shelved because I felt it would only invite more complaining and more criticism. As I ignored her and refused to talk about what she saw as our failings, she stopped bringing me her lists of grievances. And the funny thing is that, after she stopped, we slowly began to adopt nearly everything she had suggested. Not because she had complained about them, but because she stopped complaining. We made the changes because we felt they made sense. But we had held off for a long time even considering them because we had such a reaction to her demands. We had felt attacked and reacted by ignoring her requests.

You now are a more positive person talking about what you want rather than griping about what you don't want. People are going to want to work with and for you, and you will achieve and receive more than you ever dreamed. Give it time, watch for it, and it will happen.

"But what about social causes that I'm passionate about?" I'm often asked. "How can I help bring about positive change if I don't complain?" Again, change begins with dissatisfaction. It begins when someone like you sees a gap between what is and what can be. Dissatisfaction is the beginning, but it can't be the end. If you complain about a situation, you may be able to draw others to you who will bellyache along with you, but you won't be able to get much done. However, if you can begin to speak in terms of what it will be like when the challenge no longer exists, when the bridge is gapped, when the problem is solved, then you can excite and move people to positive change.

As you cease to complain, you will find yourself less often in fear and anger. Anger is fear directed outward. And because you are no longer a fear-based person, you will attract fewer angry and fearful people into your life.

In *The Seat of the Soul*, bestselling author Gary Zukav wrote, "Complaining is a form of manipulation." I have a friend who is a minister in another denomination. The sanctioning body for his religion sent a consultant to help his church grow. "Find something they're afraid of," the consultant said. "Use that to get them angry. They'll complain about the situation to others. This will unify them and draw other people in." This approach seemed out of integrity to my friend, who saw his ministry as one of serving those in need, not riling up a mob. Calling one of his fellow ministers, he asked how this fear and anger technique had worked in his church. "It worked well," the other minister said. "It brought in a lot of new people. The problem is they're a bunch of fearful and angry people who complain all the time—and now I'm stuck dealing with them." My friend resigned as senior minister of this church to become a hospital chaplain. He's living in integrity and is quite happy.

The other night, my family and I were watching the classic movie *The Music Man*, starring Robert Preston. In it, Preston plays the fast-talking, unscrupulous salesman Professor Harold Hill, who peddles band instruments.

Arriving in River City, Iowa, he asks an old friend, played by Buddy Hackett, "What is something in this town I can use to get these people upset?" Hackett tells him about the town's first pool table, which has just arrived, and Preston begins to sway the town into fear with talk of total moral corruption from pool playing. Of course, the solution to the "moral corruption" and "mass hysteria" represented by the game of pool is getting all the young men to join a band. And Professor Harold Hill is there to save the day by selling everyone band instruments and uniforms. He is fanning the flames of complaint to manipulate the townsfolk for his own profit.

Zukav is correct. Complaining is a manipulation of your energy, and now that you're a Complaint Free person, you'll notice when someone is using their negative words to try to manipulate you, and you will set up healthy boundaries to protect yourself. When you hear such talk, you know it's a complaint—with a capital C and that rhymes with T and that stands for TROUBLE.

Some say, "But some psychiatrists believe complaining is a healthy thing." As I've said, it does make sense to complain (express grief, pain, or discontent) on occasion. And an expression of grief, pain, or discontent directed toward someone who can actually help is healthy—so long as it's done in a way to receive what you want in the future and not as a means of attacking someone about the past.

Talking to a psychologist or other counselor about

challenging events in your life as a way of getting past them can be healthy. A good psychologist can give these incidents meaning and provide hope and constructive paradigms for better living in the future. However, complaining to a friend—"venting," as it's often called—can be an excuse for unbridled negativity, which draws more of our problems to us. Not to mention allies us with negative people to whom we may become entrained.

There are times when we all need to process what's going on in our lives to get a better handle on our situation. Processing and complaining are not the same thing. Processing is sharing your FEELINGS about something that has happened and not rehashing the events of what has happened. If your boss yells at you, you may want to talk to your spouse about the experience and share how it made you feel. "I felt surprised and sad when she yelled at me," you might say.

When processing an experience, make sure that what you are saying is centered on only your feelings and not your story of what happened. Use words like:

- Mad
- Sad
- Glad
- Happy
- Angry
- Afraid
- Joyous

"I feel angry when you do that" owns the experience as yours and is processing. "I feel like you're a jerk when you do that" is simply name-calling, but putting "I feel" before the attack. Your feelings are the best indicator of how well you are living in integrity with your highest self, and discussing your feelings with another, without the backstory and drama of "he said/she said," can be healthy.

Even with a therapist, it's important not to linger in the pain of any one experience for too long. One psychological study found that talking about neurotic symptoms actually increased the symptoms.* A good therapist knows how much time and energy should be devoted to the past and how to help you use what has happened to create a more desirable future.

And you are now in the driver's seat for having the future you've always dreamed of creating. More than that, by holding your intentions and speaking only of things the way you wish them to be, you will achieve goals in short order that you might have thought would take years.

In his play *Fiction,* one of Steven Dietz's characters remarks, "Writers don't like to write; they like to have written." Similarly, people don't like to change, but they like to have changed. And you've put forth the willing-

*Kowalski, R. M. (1996). "Complaints and complaining: Functions, antecedents, and consequences." *Psychological Bulletin* 119, page 181.

ness, the time, and the effort to keep switching your bracelet, starting over again and again. You are a new person. You have changed. Oliver Wendell Holmes said, "A mind stretched by a new idea never shrinks back to its original dimensions." You've made it.

If you've read this chapter and not yet completed 21 consecutive days Complaint Free, let this serve as a promise of things to come. You can do it. In the next chapter, you'll hear from people who have made 21 consecutive Complaint Free days and what it has meant to them.

CHAPTER 8

21-Day Champions

No price is too high to pay for the privilege of owning yourself.

——FRIEDRICH NIETZSCHE

B ut isn't complaining healthy?"

When I'm interviewed about the Complaint Free phenomenon, the media often want to pair me with some psychologist who espouses complaining as something that leads to better health. When this happens, I remind them that I'm not out to change people. If they want to complain, more power to them! And, just to be clear, I am not advocating remaining silent when there is something that has happened which you need corrected. Don't hold back, don't hold it in, just make sure you are only stating the facts and not putting any "how dare you do this to me?" energy behind what you are saying.

As for it being healthy, I wonder if some of these psychologists view their jobs as listening to people complain and don't want to limit their livelihood. As I've mentioned, a good therapist helps you heal traumatic events in your past by reframing and using them for a happier present and a brighter future.

I'm not a psychologist. I don't even play one on television. My experience in this arena is based solely on my own life's metamorphosis from leaving behind constant kvetching and the many people who have shared with me how much happier and healthier they have become by being Complaint Free. It seems to me that if complaining were a way to being healthy, then the people in my country, the United States, would be some of the healthiest people in the world. And yet, with what many would call the greatest medical system on planet Earth, the United States ranks below 93 percent of all other countries for heart disease deaths per capita each year. People in the United States also face challenges with high blood pressure, stroke, cancer, and other types of disease. "Dis-ease"——get it?

Michael Cunningham, Ph.D., a psychologist at the University of Louisville, proposes that the human predilection for complaining probably evolved from our ancestors' way of crying out a warning when something threatened the tribe. "We mammals are a squealing species," Dr. Cunningham says. "We talk about things that bother us as a way of getting help or seeking a posse to mount a counterattack." Rampant complaining is something we no longer need but have yet to evolve past because, as we've discussed, we still derive psychological and social benefits when we complain.

When we complain, we are saying "something is wrong." When we complain often, we live in a state of "something is wrong" and this increases stress in our lives. Imagine if someone were constantly telling you, "Beware," or "Watch out, something bad is going to happen," or "Something bad that happened in the past means more bad stuff is coming." Would it not make your life more stressful if someone were repeatedly pointing out potential dangers and pitfalls surrounding you? Of course it would. And when you complain frequently, that person sounding the warning alarm is you. You are raising your stress level by complaining. You are saying, "Something is wrong," and your body is responding with stress.

Our collective stress level reminds me of military cadets at the university I attended. Whenever one of the underclassmen would walk past an upperclassman, the cadet had to "brace." "Bracing" meant the cadet would have to bring his arms up to his sides, tuck in his chin, and tighten his whole body as if prepared for an attack. When our minds focus on what is wrong through complaining, our bodies respond. We "brace" or tighten up. Our muscles knot, our heart rate increases, our blood pressure goes up. Does this sound healthy to you?

If you look at the top-selling prescription drugs in the United States, according to a February 27, 2006, article on Forbes.com, seven of the top seven—that's right, all of them—are for illnesses that are exacerbated by stress. In 2005, $31.2 billion was spent in the United States on drugs to combat depression, heartburn, heart disease, asthma, and high cholesterol.

"Okay," you might be thinking, "I get that complaining increases stress and that heart disease, depression, and heartburn can be impacted by stress—but not asthma and high cholesterol." Well, a study by Andrew Steptoe, DSc, and colleagues from University College London, examining the effects of stress on cholesterol was detailed in *Health Psychology* (November 2005). In this experiment, Dr. Steptoe and his associates measured the cholesterol of a group of participants and then put them in stressful situations. After the stressful events, they measured each person's cholesterol and found that it had increased measurably. Stress does increase cholesterol.

As for asthma, Heather Hatfield of WebMD says, "When our anxiety [stress] levels start to creep upward . . . asthma symptoms can kick into overdrive." Stress increases asthmatic flare-ups, and complaining raises stress levels.

In my opinion, complaining is not healthy but is, in fact, detrimental to our health. But don't take my word for it; I would like to conclude this final chapter with comments from what I call "21-Day Champions"—people who have completed 21 consecutive days without complaining.

~ Joyce Cascio ~
(Author)

A year ago, if someone had asked me, "Are you someone who often complains?" I would have immediately responded, "Oh, no, not me. I rarely complain." However, the more appropriate response would have been to say, "Yes, I am someone who complains, but I am completely *unaware* just how much and how often I do it."

I was oblivious to how much I was complaining because of a 0-to-10 rating scale in my head. A 10 is someone who constantly complains and a 0 is someone who never complains. Based on this rating scale I felt I needed little improvement, because I did not see myself as a 10 or extreme complainer. I saw myself more as a middle-of-the-road complainer, maybe a 5 or, under severe circumstances, a 6. However, what I was completely missing and what my rating scale did not show me was that complaining on *any* level is harmful to me and to my relationships.

I first realized how much I was complaining during the summer of 2006. My business, which I had started in 2004, seemed to be failing. Those closest to me doubted success was possible. I felt discouraged, depressed, and negative, mostly toward myself. My conversations were exhausting because much of my energy was spent defending my position about my business and pointing out the negatives and hardships I was experiencing.

Finally, sick of all my talking, I decided to take a sabbatical in the form of a silent retreat. I needed to get away from everyone. I wrote in my journal every day, and one day in late July I began writing about the pain my own words were causing me, because many of the words I spoke did not affirm me or anyone. I realized that complaining was how I said that things were bothering me without actually saying it directly. I also used complaining as a way to create excuses for doing or not doing things. For the first time, I understood how complaining was actually robbing me of meaningful resolutions in my life. Basically, complaining was keeping me from direct and honest communication with everyone, including myself.

Ironically, the same week, unknown to me, Reverend Will Bowen was passing out Complaint Free bracelets to our congregation and asking them to go 21 days Complaint Free. When I returned a few weeks later, I was thrilled to hear about it and I immediately began wearing my bracelet.

I am happy to report that I did make it 21 days. Today, I continue to wear my bracelet as a constant reminder to myself and to support this great movement that is touching so many lives.

What has happened since completing my 21 days?

- My life is fuller, happier.
- Prospects for my business are better than ever.
- My relationships are more positive and there is less conflict in my life and relationships.

I continue to have events and circumstances that challenge me, but what has changed is how I react to those events and circumstances, and *that* is changing the outcome. Today, I am more forthright in my communication with myself and with others. Living Complaint Free has changed my life, and I know it will for anyone willing to give it a try.

~ Cathy Perry ~
(Substitute Teacher)

My twenty-first Complaint Free day was April 24. I began wearing my purple bracelet last July when Reverend Bowen first introduced the Complaint Free challenge. Over the course of the challenge, I quit and restarted several times. It took weeks just to get through one day Complaint Free. It became much easier when my husband began wearing the bracelet in October of 2006; it helps to take up the challenge with another person where you can help support each other.

This challenge helped open up my eyes to the complaining that I was doing. It was really a process of becoming aware of my thoughts and words. As soon as I realized what I was really focusing on, I was able to change my thinking about myself, about others, and about situations that I encountered every day. It's been a transformation from my daily litany of "I'm tired," "I don't get enough sleep," and "There's never enough time to get anything done" to sleeping well and feeling good.

As my focus changed, it became easier to maintain a positive attitude, and I have continued to feel better and better as the effect of positive thinking snowballed in all areas of my life. I now sleep better and have more energy. I feel happier and much more relaxed. Relationships with my family have also improved; there are more compliments than complaints in our daily conversation. Our home is such a peaceful place.

The Complaint Free challenge is not an easy one. It takes time and conscious effort to make it through that first Complaint Free day. But, once your habits and your thinking start to change, it becomes easier. The key is to keep trying.

For me, this challenge was not just about stopping complaining; it was about turning the complaints into gratitude for the blessings that I have. I see the good instead of only seeing things to complain about.

~ Don Perry ~
(Bridge Designer)

My wife started the Complaint Free challenge last July, and when she told me about it I was intrigued. I noticed a big difference in her, and in October of 2006, I started wearing one of the purple bracelets. I had it on for eight weeks before I had completed one Complaint Free day, and April 18 was my twenty-first Complaint Free day.

During this challenge, I realized how much my complaining affected my mood and how pessimistic I had become about many things. I was surprised to learn how others reacted to my negativity. One day at work, my boss asked me about my purple bracelet. When I told him about the "no complaints" challenge, he was pleased and said, "When you go on a rant, Don, you're scary." When I related this conversation to my family, they agreed that I "got scary" and oftentimes they wanted to leave the room when I "went off" while reading the paper or watching TV.

I now realize that much of my anger and complaining stems from my insecurity at my job. I would complain to anyone who would listen about the amount of work that I had or about the looming deadlines because I was just not sure that I could get it all done. And if I can't get it all done, does that mean that I'm not good enough to do the job? Consequently, I complained about it because I was fearful and angry about it. But now I realize that there's always going to be a lot of work to do, and all I can do is the best I can.

This realization has helped me come to terms with the fact that I can't control everything that happens at work or in other parts of my life and that complaining won't help the situation. I found that the less I complain about it, the less I worry about it. Letting go of that obsessive worrying has helped me enjoy time at home more and simply become more relaxed.

The Complaint Free challenge has helped me to become happier with my work relationships and at home.

My negative attitude was contagious in a poisonous way, but my new positive attitude is contagious in a healing way. The happiness it has given me has only spread. My boss calls me "Mr. Sunshine" now.

~ Marcia Dale ~
(Church Office Manager)

I've been wearing my Complaint Free Bracelet since July 23, when Reverend Will offered the challenge to our congregation to go 21 days without complaining. I thought at the time, "How hard can this be? I'm an optimistic person. I have a great family and a job I love: I work at Christ Church Unity! Twenty-one days . . . no sweat!"

Then I put on the bracelet and actually became conscious of how many negative things came out of my mouth! The awareness of that was amazing to me. Over and over I stopped myself in midsentence and asked myself, "Do I really want to continue with this statement? Is it going to accomplish anything positive?" And over and over the answer was "No." I wore out two bracelets changing wrists so often before I finally completed my 21 days in mid-November.

I continue to wear my bracelet (like a string around my finger) as a conscious reminder that my words are powerful and I have a responsibility to choose them wisely. I've realized it's not about stuffing your emotions in and putting on a Pollyanna face. I have had to deal with some difficult personal and family situations over the last several months. But before I let the words come out of my mouth, I think about them and set an intention to accomplish something positive with what I say. It is possible to deal with difficult situations (and difficult people) without becoming negative. And the result is ALWAYS so much better!

I have found that, even though I am very busy in my daily life, things seem to flow more smoothly. Some "friends" that I used to spend time with have drifted away because without something to gripe about, we don't have much to say to each other. But that opens up space for more blessings. The increased peace I feel is amazing!

~ Marty Pointer ~
(Computer Technician)

In the four months since I managed to get through 21 days without complaining, I think the greatest benefit I've noticed is easier acceptance of people who don't share my values, and of events I can't control. I don't have to work as hard now at letting things go. I find myself gently gravitating away from folks who seem to enjoy criticism and finding fault, and toward those who look for the best. A great reward has been several blossoming friendships with kindred spirits I may never have known without completing the 21-day challenge.

By finishing the 21 days, I've discovered goodness in myself that I never really believed was there. While no one behaves perfectly all the time (and I admit to an occasional relapse), I've found it so much easier to see the Light within myself after learning—as part of the 21 days—to more easily see past the imperfections in people and circumstances.

As I write this, my ninety-three-year-old mother lies in her bed at home, waiting to join her parents and many other loved ones who've gone on before her. She weighs eighty pounds and hasn't eaten for over a week. The hospice nurse says she doesn't know why Mama is still here, because all her reserves are gone. She is so weak and helpless. This situation has been very painful to me, and I was struggling to suppress my complaints toward God until I called on the many lessons I learned while doing the challenge. One of these, I recalled, was asking for help. So I asked God for help.

Yesterday I awoke with the insight that God gave my mother a wonderful, strong body that has served her in good health for ninety-three years. It has carried her to many destinations, borne and fed three babies, played musical instruments, crocheted afghans, spoken and written her thoughts, and done her will in myriad ways. That body is still faithfully trying to do its job of housing her spirit, even as it fails piece by piece. I'm now able to praise God in gratitude for this marvelous gift, and thankfully accept His plan for how the earthly part of her soul's journey ends.

While visiting with the hospice chaplain, I was able to get a personal glimpse of how the Complaint Free movement can change the world. The chaplain's eyes started shining as I explained the challenge to her, and before my explanation was even finished, she asked for fifty bracelets to give to the hospice staff. She said that although hospice workers have passion for service to the dying, they are human with all the trimmings. She thinks they will embrace the opportunity to serve better by concentrating even more on putting out only positive energy.

Six months ago, I never would have imagined how 21 days of Complaint Free living would change my life, but it truly has and now affects the lives of others around me.

~ Gary Hild ~
(Executive Chef)

My good friend Will Bowen shared his Complaint Free World process with me one day last fall as we were enjoying a beautiful afternoon riding horses near his home north of Kansas City. I was instantly intrigued with the idea. In my career as a professional chef, I feel I have to be critical—with high expectations of myself and my staff—to ensure that we consistently put out top-quality, creative food and presentation for guests with ever more sophisticated and varied palates.

Over the thirty-plus years I've lived my work life in professional kitchens, I've progressed from the old European way of tough, top-down management style to a more humane and effective coaching style. Will's new process turned out to be an idea that worked in ways I couldn't have anticipated. Specifically, after "graduating" the 21 straight days without complaining, I was so much more aware of how I communicate with my staff. I choose my words much more carefully now and think of my role more as a teacher with excellent culinary skills, rather than as a boss or manager. This frees up energy, on my part as well as others around me, to use for more enjoyable and stress-free dialogue.

I believe the Complaint Free process goes hand in hand with the Law of Attraction. My thinking and conversations are more oriented toward thankfulness and solutions, which attracts more of the same.

Today, I still wear my bracelet as a reminder and practice only one method of response to the daily workload—extreme gratefulness given in the most positive way. If I'm tempted to criticize, I stop and strive to present it more in a teaching or instructional way, and people seem to feel more appreciated and listened to. This has changed my outlook on everything and I feel freedom from stress and worry, kind of a by-product of the whole process. I am very blessed and grateful.

~ Jack Ring ~
(Clothier)

I wondered how anyone would find avoiding complaints a challenge until I began my own attempt to go 21 days without griping.

I'm in business for myself, owning a men's clothing

store. I find the business itself to be a delight. I meet a great group of people as I work with clients and the vendors whose products I sell. Many of these vendors are the designers whom we read about in fashion magazines who are bright, outgoing, and some of the most imaginative folks anyone could hope to meet.

However, as the man says, here's "the rest of the story."

Whenever people are involved with each other on a daily basis, we seem to struggle to find the best in those we deal with. Petty problems can become major events that threaten to break up relationships, provoke arguments, and at the very least wear both parties down into states of minor depression. I think we can all agree that this state of mind is unhealthy and something we would like to avoid.

I believed that I could pull off the Complaint Free 21 days, so I put on my purple bracelet. I found that, except for my business, my wife, my sons, my driving, my business partner, my employees, my suppliers, my work on a capital campaign at my church, my cats, my dog, my friends, my customers, my banker, and everyone I seemed to have contact with, I might have had a chance.

I began to notice a common thread in my problems. ME! Whenever I ran up against an obstacle to what I wanted to accomplish, I would look for something or someone to blame. I also began to notice how much I heard others complain about issues that I thought were trivial at best and in most cases prompted by actions they brought on themselves. Or they complained about things that were so far beyond their control that it seemed hopeless to complain. As I wore out bracelets by changing wrists, I began to notice how tiring it was to listen to complaints from other people and to feel grouchy myself.

The light was finally beginning to glow, and it dawned on me that my complaining was just as annoying to others as their complaints were to me. I no longer had an excuse for not making the 21 Complaint Free days. When someone else complained about something, I began to keep my mouth shut. When I had a thought of a complaint, I began to look at a possible solution or at least an acceptance of what is. On Valentine's Day, while on a buying trip with my business partner and our wives, I finally made my 21 days.

One of the differences it has made in my life occurred when I realized that as I stopped complaining I heard less complaining from those around me. If I heard complaints, I understood that they weren't directed at me but were attempts by others to understand the events taking place in their lives. I have also become less judgmental toward others. Looking for solutions or acceptance has led to my feeling less stress and accomplishing more at home and at work. My relationships with my wife, family, and associates improved as my grouchiness lessened. I am a happier person.

By keeping quiet during outbursts from other people, I give them no audience and allow them to reflect on their comments. We can say that it takes two to make a complaint, just as it takes two to make an argument. The purple bracelet can help even those who don't choose to wear it. Without an audience, we find ourselves more attuned to dealing with the problems at hand and getting on with our lives.

Keeping our complaints quiet can be compared to the silence of meditation; it's easier to hear God talk to us.

~ Rick Silvey ~
(College Professor)

If someone would have told me when I embarked upon this adventure that it would take so long to complete, I wouldn't have believed them. For you see, I've never really considered myself a gossip or complainer; sarcastic maybe, but not a complainer. But once I focused my attention on my behavior, I realized that an incident of complaint would "rear its ugly head" just often enough to prevent me from successfully completing the program.

So, armed with spiritual practices that I have collected along my journey, I set out to eradicate complaining completely from my life. Three times each day I gave thanks for a Complaint Free experience and I envisioned how that experience would manifest itself. I also used positive affirmations and quotes to inspire me throughout the day. My objective was to transfer the undesirable traits that had become embedded into my unconsciousness to my consciousness, where I could begin the work to remove them. I believe this is an integral part of the process. Until I became aware that I possessed and exhibited these traits, I could not begin to eradicate them. Slowly but surely, I was able release these incidents of complaint and gossip with greater ease.

This exercise in becoming Complaint Free has strengthened my optimistic outlook on life. I am more aware how negative thinking hinders my ability to be at peace with myself and others. I have witnessed an improvement in my relationships with my partner, family, colleagues, and students. I am more patient and experience less urgency in all my affairs. While politicians continue to provide me with opportunities for spiritual growth, I find myself more relaxed and emotionally detached from their behaviors. Don't get me wrong, I still stand firm in my beliefs, but I am able to communicate my position in ways that are nobler.

I have decided to extend this exercise for another 21 days. This time—in addition to abstaining from complaining, gossiping, and sarcasm—I'll focus on eliminating thoughts of insecurity and doubt. In the future, I may continue to add other self-defeating, negative thoughts so that I can truly model the Christ Spirit in all that I think, say, and do.

This experience is, for me, best summed up in this quote from George Bernard Shaw, "Life is no brief candle to me; it is a sort of splendid torch, which I've got a hold of for the moment and I want to make it burn as brightly as possible before handing it on to future generations." Becoming a Complaint Free person ourselves raises the bar and sets a new standard for future generations.

~ Tom Alyea ~
(Business Consultant and Senior Coordinator of
A Complaint Free World)

As a fan of the old *I Love Lucy* shows, I used to love it when Ricky Ricardo walked through the door each day and shouted, "Hi, Lucy, I'm home." For the first years of my marriage, I would do the same: "Hi, Mischa, I'm home." But at some point in my life it got to be a lot easier to say, "Hi, Mischa, I'm home and my head [or back, feet, or stomach] hurts."

Complaining had become a way a life for me, a way to get attention, a way to get my point across, a way to just open a conversation. I always saw myself as such a positive, happy person. That was until I came home from church one Sunday in July 2006 and told my wife about this 21-day challenge to stop complaining. Here I was all excited, and I was telling her I was going to be the first to make the 21 days in the congregation. She just smiled and said, "Twenty-one days—I'd like to see you go 21 minutes without complaining." And, about six minutes later, I realized that this was going to be the challenge of a lifetime. My wife and I were sitting on the couch and all of a sudden I said, "Wow, it's really hot outside and it sure is making my head hurt." She looked at me, then looked at my bracelet (which I switched right then and there— twice, because I complained two times in just one sentence!). The truth is that the silence in those six minutes was driving me nuts and I had to open a conversation with something. I wanted attention and thought that was the best way to get it.

So that was my first challenge—learn how to start a conversation without a complaint. Once I worked on that, then I moved on to other complaints. The kids' rooms are a mess—tell me, does complaining about a teenager's room every really get it cleaned any faster? The weather—what can I do about it? And the list went on and on as the number of complaints went down and down, and as I realized just how negative these thoughts and words were to me and others.

After spending five months working on the 21-day challenge, I finally made it! Do I have fewer headaches? Yes, because I realized I didn't have too many of them in the first place. What I see now is a body that is healthy and whole and is working on healing all the time. Am I happier? You betcha! Dinners with the kids are a lot nicer when talk is less about complaining about dirty rooms and more about their hopes and dreams. Am I glad I persevered and made it the 21 days? Short of a wonderful marriage, and three kids whom I love and adore, this has been the best thing to happen in my life, ever.

~ Catherine Bohm ~
(Nurse)

When I received my bracelet, I soon discovered that going a whole day without complaining was very difficult. Weekends went well, then came Monday and a workday. Even though I dearly love my job, it does have organizational and administrative issues like any job.

After five months, I saw people receiving a "Certificate of Happiness" and I really got determined. I asked all my coworkers to assist me by refraining from complaining, to keep me from wanting to join in. Everyone was so good; if they looked to me to join in a negative conversation, I would tug on my bracelet and we would change the subject.

Things were going well nearing the two-week mark. After an especially difficult day, I realized I had not brought the doctor group into my little plan when one of the doctors really got under my skin. The following day, all the RNs were to drive across town to assist in moving the entire company of medical records from the old to the new computer system without instruction on how to accomplish this. It was a hard task, and after we finished three of us went to lunch and complained for two hours.

This lunch restarted my 21 days—again. When I reached 20 days on the next try, I arrived at work and in walked a nurse who did not like me and would not talk to me when we worked together. Then the very same doctor who had made me lose it on day 14 of the previous attempt walked in. Only one day to go and I stood face-to-face with my two greatest challenges. I laughed and said, "God, You have the greatest sense of humor, and I accept." I not only made it without complaining, that turned out to be one of the best days I've ever had at work.

~ Patricia Platt ~
(Teacher)

I began my endeavor to go 21 days thinking, "This will be easy! I don't complain much—and I live by myself." Well, it took me nearly four months to accomplish this goal!

As a young girl, I was sexually abused by my father and an uncle. As a way to cope with the abuse, I turned to alcohol, drugs, and unhealthy relationships. Over eighteen years ago, I got clean and began to heal from the abuse. However, I continued to struggle with thoughts of low self-worth and depression. I didn't know how to stop the negative thinking. I had tried affirmations, therapy, and self-help books. People would tell me, "Just don't think that way," but I didn't know how to stop. Striving for a Complaint Free life has finally freed me!

When I first began this process, I had to switch my bracelet many times in a day. Then I could make it a couple, and then I could go 7 days, then about 14. I had gotten stuck when an article about the movement was published in our local paper. Several of my students told me their parents had seen my name in the paper and wanted to know why. I shared the article and they wanted to try it. Well, having twenty-five fourth-graders watching me got me unstuck!

One of the difficulties I faced during this process was due to my increased awareness of the amount of negativity expressed by others. I felt angry and judgmental. There were times when I wanted to hide, but that wasn't always an option, nor would it help me learn to deal with the problem. So I learned to be a better listener. I worked at listening to the message the person was sending behind their words. For example, when a coworker would complain about their class, rather than chiming in or sitting silently, I would offer comments such as "It sounds like a very frustrating situation. When I've had things like that happen, this is what I've tried." As I continued to work through this challenge, I began to realize that the quality of my relationships improved.

But by far the greatest gift I have received is the freedom from depression! The joy and contentment I feel on a daily basis has given me the peace I prayed and searched for since I was a young girl. Sure, I have moments where I become frustrated with life, but rather than complain, I thank God for the gifts the situation is giving me. And since I choose not to whine, I remind myself of my definition of love: unconditional acceptance and looking for the good.

Do any of the Champions' comments resonate with you? Did you find in their stories a change or improvement you would like to see in your own life? You can make this your reality by systematically removing rampant complaining from your life. By moving your bracelet over and over until you succeed, you WILL succeed.

Uva Uvam Videndo Varia Fit

Complaining is not to be confused with
informing someone of a mistake or deficiency
so that it can be put right. And to refrain from
complaining doesn't necessarily mean putting up
with bad quality or behavior. There is no ego in
telling the waiter your soup is cold and needs to
be heated up—if you stick to the facts, which
are always neutral. "How dare you serve me cold
soup . . . ?" That's complaining.*

—ECKHART TOLLE, A NEW EARTH

The best summary for this book comes from the
quote by Eckhart Tolle that begins this chapter.
Directing a comment to someone who can improve your
situation is not complaining. Berating someone or

*Tolle, Eckhart (2005). *A New Earth*, page 63.

lamenting the situation either to yourself or to another is complaining. And complaining draws more of what you don't want to you.

If you verbally attack a waiter for cold soup, he may return with hot soup, but who's to say what he may have added to your bowl in his anger—possibly things you don't want to know about. When a person is complained to or criticized, they feel attacked and their first response is often to defend themselves. This defense may present itself in the form of a counterattack. Even if this does not occur, in your complaining you have sent out vibrations to the Universe of your being a victim and, in so doing, have invited more victimizers to you.

Complaining is often a means of drawing attention to one's self. Everyone desires to be recognized, but people who complain a lot may be trying to attract attention because of low self-esteem. They may complain to those around them as a way of demonstrating their discriminating tastes and sophistication, especially when they feel unsure about themselves in these areas. They may also complain to legitimize and concretize self-appointed limitations to excuse themselves from stretching, growing, and improving their lives.

A complaint may be a cry for attention, but it is also a signal to the Universe that something is wrong. The Universe, being both beneficent and neutral, then sends more "wrong." When someone complains about something, they are unknowingly placing an order to receive more to complain about, and the negative spiral perpetuates.

The way out is to stop complaining and to express gratitude when positive things happen. In every life, there are many, many things about which to be grateful. To remind myself of this, as soon as I wake up each day, I write down five things for which I am grateful. I have found that rather than just think about what I'm appreciative of, if I write them down, it sets a tone of gratitude for my entire day.

What you articulate, you demonstrate. Talk about negative and unhappy things and you will receive negative and unhappy things. Talk about things for which you are grateful and you will draw more things to you that are enjoyable. You have a habitual pattern of speaking that demonstrates what you are thinking, and this is creating your daily reality. Whether you realize it or not, you plot your course each day and then follow that course. The results can be pleasant or painful.

When I was a child, one of the stories my mother used to tell me was about a baker, a stranger, and a miserly shopkeeper. In this story, one of my favorites as a child, the stranger enters a small village seeking food and shelter for the night. When asked if they will help the traveler, the miserly shopkeeper and his wife turn the man away.

The stranger then walks into the bakery. The baker is penniless and nearly out of baking supplies. Nonetheless, he invites the man in and shares a meager meal with him. Then the baker gives the man his own bed in which to sleep. The next morning, the stranger thanks the baker and tells him, "Whatever you do first this morning, you will continue all day."

The baker is unsure as to the meaning of this strange comment. Nonetheless, he decides to bake his guest a cake to take with him. Surveying the last of his supplies, he finds two eggs, a cup of flour, and some sugar and spices. He begins to bake. To the baker's surprise, the more supplies he uses, the more supplies there are. As he draws out the last two eggs, he notices four more in their place. He tips the flour sack to shake out the last cup of flour, and the sack is full when he sets it down. Overjoyed with his good luck, the baker throws himself into baking all manner of delicacies and soon the town square is filled with the delicious aroma of baked breads, cookies, cakes, and pies. Customers line up around the block to purchase his creations.

That evening, tired, happy, and his cash register overflowing, the baker is approached by the miserly shopkeeper. "How did you get so many customers today?" the shopkeeper demands. "It seemed like everyone in town bought baked goods from you—some more than once." The baker shares the story of the stranger he had helped as well as the man's strange blessing that morning.

The shopkeeper and his wife run from the bakery and down the road out of town. They run until, at last, they find the man they had refused help the night before. "Gentle sir," they say. "Please forgive our rudeness last night. We must have been out of our heads not to have helped you. Please, return with us to our home and allow us the honor of sharing our hospitality with you." Without a word, the man joins them on the road back into town.

When they arrive at the shopkeeper's home, the traveler is fed a sumptuous meal with fine wine and delicious confections for dessert. He sleeps in a luxurious room on a bed of goose down. The next morning, as the man is preparing to leave, the shopkeeper and his wife bounce up and down on their toes in anticipation, waiting for him to cast his magic spell over them. Sure enough, the stranger thanks his hosts and says, "Whatever you do first this morning, you will continue all day."

Rushing the stranger out the door, the shopkeeper and his wife dash to their store. Expecting a large number of customers that day, the shopkeeper grabs a broom and begins to sweep the floor to prepare for the onslaught of traffic. Wanting to make sure they have enough change for the purchases certain to happen that day, the wife begins to count the change in the till. He sweeps and she counts. She counts and he sweeps. Try as they might, they cannot stop sweeping and counting until the day is over.

Both the baker and the shopkeeper received the same blessing. The baker begins his day in a positive and generous way and receives great abundance. The shopkeeper begins his day in a negative and self-serving way and derives nothing. The blessing is neutral. Your ability to create your life is neutral. Use it however you wish; you will reap what you sow.

And remember that when someone critically lashes out at you, they are doing so from their own fear and insecurities. They are coming from what they feel is a weak position and amplify their vitriol as a way of making themselves appear big and strong when they actually feel small and weak. They are projecting their fear and discomfort onto others. They attempt to hurt because they are hurting.

If we want to improve the world, it must first come from our healing the discord within our own souls. Changing our words will ultimately change our thoughts, which will, in turn, change our world. When we cease complaining, we remove the primary outlet for our negative thoughts, our minds shift, and we become happier. Having no place for the negative thoughts to be expressed, the mind ceases production of them. When your mouth stops expressing negative thoughts, your mind will find other, happier thoughts to create. The thought factory that is your mind is always producing, and in the absence of a customer for negativity, it will retool and produce happy thoughts.

Our outer worlds are a projection of our inner worlds. Our relationship with another begins with our relationship with ourselves. You can't treat others any better than you treat yourself. It all begins with you. In Matthew 7:3,

Jesus said, "Why do you look at the speck of sawdust in your brother's eye and pay no attention to the plank in your own eye?" If you are noticing a great number of people around you complaining, you might want to look in your own eye and do a quick plank-check.

When you complete your 21 consecutive days Complaint Free, you move from being a person who is addicted to complaining to being one who is in recovery from a complaining addiction. Alcoholics say that no matter how long they've been sober, if they spend enough time around booze, they are going to drink. If people around you are complaining, look inside yourself to see if you have drawn these people to you. If, when you have become a Complaint Free person, they persist, extricate yourself from them. If they are at your place of work, change departments or change jobs—the Universe will support you along your positive new path. If they are friends, you may realize that you have evolved beyond the present relationship. Even if they are family members, it may be best to limit your experiences with them.

Don't allow people who are negative to rob you of the life you seek. It takes 21 days to form a habit. You can reverse the Complaint Free habit with 21 days of your old behavior, so be aware of those around you, because you may be tempted to follow their lead. Take care of yourself and beware of toxic, complaining people. If you don't take care of yourself, you could sink back into the mire of negativity. And remember that your stepping back from a complaining person may be just the motivation he or she needs to examine their life and grow.

The best way to help others is to model Complaint Free living. As you do, love those around you. The best definition of "love" I've ever found comes from Dr. Denis Waitley: "Love is unconditional acceptance and looking for the good." As we accept other people and situations and look for the good in them, we will experience more and more goodness, because our focus draws this expression into our reality. This means we don't try and get others to stop complaining. Rather, we become Complaint Free ourselves and hold a vision of our lives without complaint or complaining people. Our vibrations will attract happy, healthy people to us, and those who are not this type of person will feel uncomfortable around us and they will move on.

Using old phrases in new ways is essential to living a Complaint Free life. When something good happens, no matter how small, say to yourself, "Of course!", knowing that you are a magnet for beneficence. You might even put a knowing smile on your face to anchor the experience. Did you find a parking place right in front of the store you're visiting on a rainy day? Say, "Just my luck!" Did you forget to put money in the parking meter and return to find no ticket under your windshield wiper? Affirm, "This always happens to me." If someone gets in your face about something, say, "Thank you for teaching me compassion." As you begin this it may feel silly, but every time you use powerful, affirmative words for your experiences, you are putting solid bricks into a foundation of more joy and abundance.

People have used the term "fad" when talking to me about the Complaint Free purple bracelets. In his book *How to Create Your Own Fad*, Ken Hakuta defines a fad as "something everyone wants today and no one wants tomorrow." If that's the case, then the purple bracelets may be a fad. Certainly, judging by the thousands of requests we receive daily, everyone seems to want them today. When people ask me when I think the requests will reach their limit, I usually respond, "As soon as we hit six billion"— that is, one for every person on the planet. Actually, it may never be that large. The purple bracelets may someday be a trivia question for the first decade of the twenty-first century. But becoming Complaint Free is not a fad; it is a shift in human consciousness that is here to stay. The genie is out of the bottle, and the world will never be the same thanks to this simple and yet profound idea.

We are currently working with children's psychologists to create Complaint Free school programs and curricula for children. We are working on Complaint Free relationship models, Complaint Free workplaces, Complaint Free churches, and much more. Our current goal is to encourage the leaders of the countries around the world to proclaim one day a year as "Complaint Free." Not a holiday, but a day like the "Great American Smoke-Out" here in the United States. A day for people to taste what it would be like to leave behind complaining, criticizing, and gossiping. In the United States and in Canada, there is a move afoot to designate this day as the day before Thanksgiving. It only makes sense: You spend a day free of complaining and move directly into a day of gratitude. The opposite of complaining IS gratitude. If you are so moved, contact your senator, congressperson, member of Parliament, president, or other leader in your country and bang the drum to make this happen. Let's raise the awareness of the transformational power when a country and its people focus their incredible collective energy on solutions rather than problems.

In Larry McMurtry's novel *Lonesome Dove*, one of the lead characters, a pseudo-intellectual cowboy named Gus McCrae, carves a Latin motto into the bottom of the sign for his livery business. The motto reads, "Uva Uvam Vivendo Varia Fit." McMurtry does not explain the motto and actually misspells it—as a way, I presume, of showing the cowboy's poor grasp of Latin. The correct spelling is "Uva Uvam Videndo Varia Fit." The phrase means that one grape changes color when it sees another. Put another way: One grape ripens another.

In a vineyard, one grape will begin to ripen and in so doing will send out a vibration, an enzyme, a fragrance, or an energy field of some kind that is picked up by the other grapes. This one grape signals the other grapes that it is time to change, to ripen. As you become a person who holds only the highest and best for yourself and others in your words and thoughts, you will signal to all around you simply by who you are that it is time for a change. Without even trying, you will raise the consciousness of those around you.

Entrainment is a powerful principle. I think this is why human beings like to hug one another. When we hug, even for just a brief second, our hearts entrain and we remind ourselves that there is only one life on this planet. One life we all share.

If we don't choose how we live our version of this one life with intention, we will live it by default, following along after others. We often follow along after others without even realizing we are doing so. When my father was a young man, he managed a motel owned by my grandfather. The motel was across the street from a used-car lot, and my dad worked out an arrangement with the owner of the car dealership. On evenings when the motel's business was slow, my father would go over and move a dozen or so cars from the dealership into the motel parking lot. In a short time, the motel would be full of paying customers. The people passing the motel reasoned that if the lot was empty, the motel must not be very good. However, if the motel's parking lot was full, the passersby figured it must be a good place to stay. We follow others. And you have now become a person who is leading the world toward peace, understanding, and abundance for all.

Last night, I was awakened around 3 A.M. by coyotes howling in our pasture. The howling began with one, lone coyote pup and spread among the pack. In a very short time, our two dogs, Gibson and Magic, picked up the howling. Soon, our neighbors' dogs began to howl and the howling crept up the valley in every direction as dogs all around us joined in. The coyotes had created a ripple that was spreading. After a while, I could hear howling dogs in every direction from miles away, and it all began with just one small coyote pup.

Who you are creates an impact on your world. In the past, your impact may have been negative because of your propensity to complain. Now, however, you are modeling optimism and a better world for all. You are a ripple in the great ocean of humanity that resounds around the world.

You are a blessing.